The Faith-Work Connection

The Faith-Work Connection

A Practical Application
of Christian Values
in the Workplace

Graham Tucker

Anglican Book Centre
Toronto, Canada

1987
Anglican Book Centre
600 Jarvis Street
Toronto, Ontario
Canada M4Y 2J6

Copyright © 1987 by Anglican Book Centre

All rights reserved. No part of this book may be reproduced, stored in a retrieval system, or transmitted, in any form or by any means, electronic, mechanical photocopying, recording, or otherwise, without the written permission of the Anglican Book Centre.

Typesetting by Jay Tëe Graphics Ltd.

Canadian Cataloguing in Publication Data

Tucker, Graham.
  The faith-work connection

Bibliography: p.

ISBN 0-919891-60-8

1. Management - Religious aspects - Christianity.
2. Christian life - Anglican authors. I. Title.

HD38.T82 1987   658   C87-093280-2

Contents

    Introduction 7
1 A World in Transition 12
2 The Unshakable Kingdom 20
3 The Power of Values 35
4 Values in the Workplace 50
5 Value-Based Management 68
6 Community in the Workplace 88
7 Business Ethics and Social Responsibility 102
8 Creative Problem Solving 116
9 The Ministry of the Laity 133
10 A Strategy for Lay Ministry 146
Appendices 162
Notes 216
Bibliography 221

*To the friends of the King Bay Chaplaincy
who have shared in the learning process
and the discovery of the connection
between faith and work.*

Introduction

Ministry in the World

For the past eight years I have had the exciting experience of developing a new form of ministry to the business community in Toronto, a city of over two million people and the financial centre of Canada. The result of that ministry is the King-Bay Chaplaincy which empowers and supports the laity in the workplace. I discovered, somewhat to our surprise, that the timeless values which underlie the biblical faith give it the potential of providing the basis for the most effective and responsible method of managing the human and material resources of the world. This book is based on that discovery and on my insights from a varied career in both the church and the business world.

I began my career as a mechanical engineer interested in the practical business of designing machines and building manufacturing plants. However, through the example and witness of two young engineers who were dedicated Christians, my life was turned around to following the Christ who claimed to be "the way, the truth, and the life." This led to my ordination in the Anglican church, and my life shifted from applied science to applied Christianity.

Having been led to a spiritual awakening through the influence of two laymen in the workplace rather than in the institutional church, I have a strong bias towards the development and empowerment of the ministry of the laity. I believe this will be the major strength of the church in the future. This belief has shaped my ministry, and this book attempts to bridge the serious gap which exists between the institutional church and the workplace, and the world of business and commerce in particular.

It is also designed to provide guidelines for those men and women who find themselves caught up in the pressures, anxieties, and opportunities of the business world, but who want to remain true to their faith in that context. It is for those who believe that God is the sovereign Lord of the universe, including the secular world, and who would like to be agents of change for God in the workplace, but are not sure how to go about it.

I have been influenced by the writings of William Diehl, an engineer and former sales manager for the Bethlehem Steel Corporation and an active Lutheran layman. In his book *Christianity and Real Life*, he focuses on the gap between our Sunday faith and our weekday world. He points out how little practical support, encouragement, and training the church gives to lay people to equip them for their ministry in the world. Most of what is called lay training in the church is designed to enable people to function more effectively within the structure of the church in such roles as teaching, leading worship, visiting members, serving on committees, and giving time and money to the organization. These are good and necessary activities, but they do not equip people for ministry in the world. William Diehl writes, "I am not alone in my disillusionment. On the basis of personal conversations as well as surveys conducted by the churches themselves it is obvious to me that many other lay people feel that the church has all but abandoned them in their weekday world."[1]

A Personal Journey of Faith

Following my ordination, I was anxious to combine my training as an engineer and a clergyman. This led into a pioneer ministry as one of the few *worker-priests* in North America. I was commissioned to start a church in Kitimat, British Columbia, in what was then one of the largest hydroelectric projects in the world. While building a congregation and establishing a church, I worked as a construction and industrial engineer.

I learned many lessons in my ten years of that pioneer ministry. I learned why the worker-priest movement was phased out by the church in Europe. There is very little that an ordained worker in business or industry can do that could not be done by a committed Christian lay person. Both must do the job they are being paid to do with integrity. And in the work context faith is not appropriately expressed in theological language, it is better manifested in one's relationships, values, attitudes, leadership style, and concern for people. This Christian lifestyle in the workplace will be the focus of the following chapters.

I also learned the power of a co-operative community. When a group of people with a common faith and a common purpose meet regularly as a caring and sharing community, they can accomplish a great deal. It is interesting to note that such widely read books on modern management as *In Search of Excellence* by T.J. Peters and R.H. Waterman and *Corporate Culture* by T. Deal and A. Kennedy indicate that the building of a strong sense of community within a company is one of the most important ingredients for its success as a creative and productive organization. I began to study the dynamics of building an intentional and productive community, for I believe that the twentieth-century church should be extensively involved in this type of ministry. The church has been in the business of building community for two thousand years, and although congregations often fail to function as effective communities, we do have a great depth of experience. When this experience is combined with the modern psychological insights of group dynamics and human relations, it can help Christian managers and employees to transform and humanize the workplace.

The next stage of my career involved a position at the national office of the Anglican church, responsible for stewardship teaching, training, and programming. I learned that stewardship is one of the most powerfully relevant theological concepts for the modern world. It concerns our responsible management of all the resources of the earth for the good of all people, according to the will and purpose of the real owner, who is God. The stewardship way of looking at things is one of the best ways I know of providing sound guidelines to the business, industrial, and political decision makers who are responsible for managing the resources of the earth. They must be held accountable for waste, pollution, depletion of forests without renewal, and the misuse of atomic fission to kill and destroy when it could be used to bless the earth with abundant energy.

Many issues boil down to questions of economics. The Greek word *oikos* meaning "house" or "household" plus a derivative of the word *nemein* meaning to "manage" together form *oikonomia*

oikonomia which is the basis of our word "economy." It is interesting to note that the Greek word *oikonomia* is the common root for the words "stewardship," "management," and "economics." It literally means the management or regulation of the household affairs, with special regard for costs and in accordance with the will of the owner.

In biblical usage the word *oikonomia* is translated "stewardship." It is related to God's plan for the universe, the "divine economy." We are accountable to God for the responsible management of the human and material resources of the earth. Stewardship is thus a basic element of the Christian life. However, because the church is often preoccupied with its own life and development, it has neglected to get the stewardship concepts of Christianity into society and the workplace. This requires a translation of biblical concepts and values into terms of everyday life and decision making.

The next stage of my career prepared me for the job of translation. As director of the Aurora Conference Centre in the diocese of Toronto for eight years, I was involved in the development of a wide variety of educational programs for both clergy and laity. It was a great opportunity to be able to think and reflect upon the relationship of the Christian faith to a rapidly changing modern world. I asked myself, "What difference does it make to be a Christian today? Should we be different in any significant way from those who do not share a faith in Jesus Christ as Lord?" The result of this quest was the publication of my first book *It's Your Life — Create a Christian Lifestyle*.[2] In it I concluded that our personal value system determines our choices and actions. Our values are formed in a variety of places: mainly in the home, but also in such places as the church and our social and work groups. However, unless we have the considerable inner strength required to maintain a consistent lifestyle, particularly when it runs counter to the prevailing culture, we are likely to compromise and adapt. For example, we may live by one set of values on weekends when we relate to family and church, but by a different set of values Monday to Friday at work. It is one of the aims of this book to find ways of dealing helpfully and creatively with this schizophrenia.

The King-Bay Chaplaincy

The past nine years as director of the ecumenical King-Bay Chaplaincy have provided me with an opportunity to intregate and apply many of these insights. The Chaplaincy has two offices, a chapel, and a meeting room. They are in a major office tower in the Wall Street district of Canada. It is a pioneer ministry, with no guidelines and no built-in support system or congregation. We see ourselves as a research and development arm of the churches, scouting out the land to find a way for others to follow. Having found some ways which work, we thought it wise to put our findings into a book which shares practical insights with those who are so often urged from the pulpit to "be the church in the world" but seldom are given any help in how to do it. (See Appendix 1 for further information on the business ministry of King-Bay Chaplaincy.)

1
A World in Transition

Powerful forces are revolutionizing life on this planet. Decades from now, the 1980s will be remembered as a time when the world accelerated toward a new age. New York Times

Shaping the Future

Many best sellers have been written about the world's acceleration towards a new age, and the scenarios range from an atomic holocaust to a golden age. The futurists write as if the future already exists and we have only to wait for it to arrive. They extrapolate the present into the future. The future is not like that; it is open ended, and we are creating it right now by our choices, decisions, and actions. What we decide to do about the national debt now will determine the kind of burden that future generations will have to bear. Our decisions now about unemployment and nuclear weapons, trade barriers and free enterprise are shaping the new age.

One of the encouraging trends identified by John Naisbitt in his book *Megatrends* is that as people begin to lose faith in the decision makers in the political and economic realms, they begin to take more responsibility at local levels, and they begin to discover that power is no longer simply money in the hands of a few, but information in the hands of many. Despite media bias and distortion, the average person has greater access to information than ever before, and information is power. When we process information through our value system we can begin to make intelligent choices which will shape the future. The key questions are: ==What kind of values do we bring to this process and how can we apply them more fully? That's what this book is about.==

I believe that those who hold and profess Christian convictions have an urgent responsibility to clarify their own values, envision a future based on biblical principles, and then give the kind of leadership which will make that future a reality. Surely this was our Lord's intention when he taught his followers to pray, "Thy kingdom come on earth, as it is in heaven." From a Christian perspective the problem is the difficulty of maintaining a spiritual faith in a secular world, and the ideal is the kingdom of God on earth.

The Problem of Faith in the Modern World

After many years of ministry within the context of the church, moving into an office on the twelfth floor of a skyscraper was something of a culture shock. It was was if I had moved into another world, in which all reminders of the presence of God had been removed. When one lives and works within the context of the church, there are constant reminders, from the architecture of the buildings to the symbol of the cross. But in the concrete canyons of the business district the towering monuments of glass and steel point only to the power of man. And so I learned what it feels like to be a Christian in a totally secular environment.

The sense of isolation was made easier to bear by the presence of my secretary, Mrs. Ruth Cartwright, a dedicated and theologically trained lady who has shared in the development of the business ministry. As we sat there on the first day wondering how to begin, we decided that when all else fails you read the instructions, so we began each day with Bible study and prayer.

We were soon struck with the centrality of the kingdom of God in the preaching and teaching of Jesus. He said, "Seek ye first the kingdom of God, and his righteousness; and all these things shall be added unto you."[1] And of course he told his followers to pray that God's kingdom would come on earth as it is in heaven. But what did the kingdom of God have to do with the great office towers surrounding us? We began to feel as if our office on the twelfth floor was an outpost in alien territory.

In recent history the church seems to have laboured under the impression that God's concerns are largely confined to the church and the sanctuary. However, the New Testament picture of Jesus and his ministry was of a man who spent most of his time, not in the temple or synagogue, but in the world, among tax collectors, business people, fishermen, the sick, and the outcast. The incarnate Lord saw all of life in relationship to his Father, and his primary business was the inauguration of the kingdom of God on earth. In the light of Jesus' approach to ministry, I believe that the church's exclusive emphasis on the parish or congregational ministry is a parochial captivity which could profoundly affect its future.

The church must develop all kinds of new ministries which support and empower the laity in the incredibly difficult task of applying the values, attitudes, and perspectives of the kingdom of God to the almost totally secular kingdom of man. The problem is that the people of God are visible in church on Sunday and practically invisible in the workplace Monday to Friday. Thus the message tends to be that Christianity is largely irrelevant to the real world of daily life.

I believe that this message of irrelevance is one of the major reasons for the present crisis of faith. The indications are that despite a widespread and vague belief in God, the vast majority of Canadians have little connection with any religion. They will not accept the Christian faith as the central influence in their lives if it does not relate significantly to the workplace, where most of life is spent. If God is not the sovereign Lord of all of life, including the workplace, then he is not Lord at all.

The Conflicting Kingdoms

We live in the overlap between two kingdoms — the kingdom of God and the kingdom of man. The whole New Testament is about the struggle between these two kingdoms and their radically different value systems. One can only understand the ministry of Jesus in the light of this conflict.

A World in Transition 15

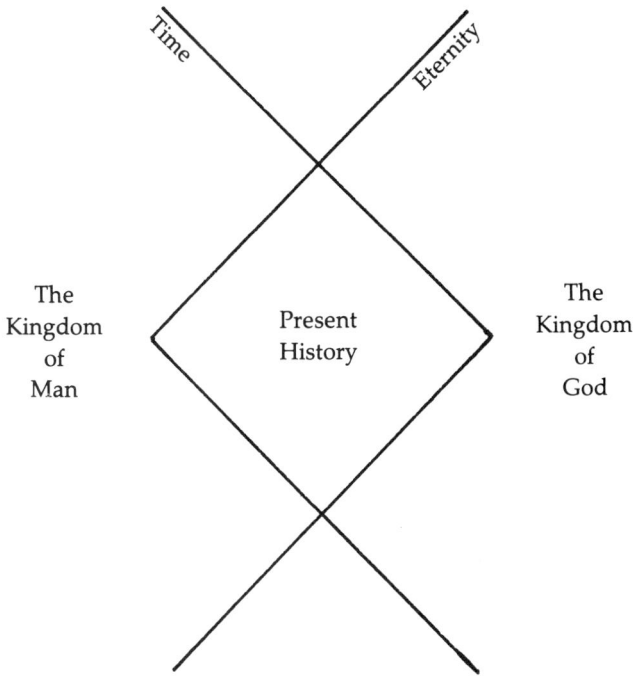

During the time between the first and second comings of Christ, the local churches are meant to be outposts of the kingdom of God battling in the midst of the kingdom of man. The Roman empire spread its culture by establishing city colonies as outposts in occupied territory. Saint Paul saw the relationship of the church to the secular world as similar; Christians were ambassadors from a different culture and value system. Thus the role of the local church is to manifest the culture of Christ to penetrate and change the culture of our society. It should be the community in which, through the ministry of the word and the sacraments, the universal message of sin and forgiveness, grace and redemption, peace, love, and co-operative community are lived and proclaimed into the everyday life of the world. But the church seems to have taken out citizenship in the kingdom of man. It is quite at home in a materialistic and self-centred culture. Unfortunately we have largely lost the capacity to "think Christianly" and now tend to "think secularly" with materialistic categories which ignore spiritual realities. Contrary to Saint Paul's warning, we have become "conformed to this world" and have not renewed our minds with the mind of Christ. In his book *The Christian Mind*, Harry Blamires says, "We twentieth-century Christians have chosen the way of compromise. We withdraw our Christian consciousness from the fields of public, commercial, and social life. When we enter these fields we are compelled to accept for purposes of discussion the secular frame of reference established there . . . . We have no Christian vocabulary to match the complexities of contemporary political, social, and industrial life."[2]

How did such a serious gap between the institutional church and the workplace come about and what can we do about it?

The gap did not develop overnight. It has been developing for the past two hundred years since the Enlightenment, the intellectual movement of the eighteenth century which asserted that the laws of nature rather than God are supreme. It was felt that man was perfectable if he would only follow the laws of nature. Adam Smith, the father of modern capitalism, based his economic theory on the assumption that if everyone acted on the basis of self-interest, some unseen providential hand would bring about an equilibrium in the marketplace which would be to the benefit of all. This led to the belief that economic life is a natural impersonal system which functions apart from any moral considerations. Moral accountability is removed from those who make business decisions and the rubric "business is business" becomes the *modus operandi*.

The consequences of this cultural perspective are manifold. Moral dualism, in which one's private and personal life is expected to be governed by moral laws while one's business life is dictated by economic expediency, has provided a convenient rationale for many Christian people. It avoids the costly struggle for justice and compassion in the marketplace and makes it easy to adopt a Machiavellian philosophy in which the end justifies the means; and the end is usually the economic bottom line. We put property rights above personal rights, technological development above human development, competition above cooperation, and economic values above human values.

Most of us have grown up taking this situation for granted, or at least as an unfortunate but inevitable state of affairs. But now, I believe, we are in a time of spiritual awakening which calls us to see all of life as an integrated whole.

In spite of its many weaknesses and failings, I believe that our modified free enterprise system is still better than all of the alternatives, simply because it is based on freedom rather than coercion. What I am advocating is that Christians cease to accept moral dualism and reaffirm the sovereignty of God over all of life, which is precisely what Jesus meant by the kingdom of God on earth. We have to learn how to apply Christian values in all areas of life, including the workplace. If we do not bridge the gap between church and society, the moral power of the gospel will fade away with an irrelevant church.

Speaking at a public meeting sponsored by the King-Bay Chaplaincy, Malcolm Muggeridge referred to the many crises facing the world. He said, "What we are suffering from is not an unemployment crisis, or energy crisis, or political crisis, or food crisis — but from a loss of a moral order in the universe." One of the dilemmas of a secular society is how to construct a moral and ethical system without reference to God. Because of the evident decline of moral standards in our society, and the apparent failure of parents to handle the difficult job of values education, the school systems are attempting to undertake the task. However, the public school system is secular and is not allowed to develop a God-centred value system. Without reference to God, one ends up with a philosophy of hedonism in which happiness is the highest good, and all values become relative; there are no ultimate values. Where can we find a sane and sound value system and the power by which to live it? The Lord's Prayer points to the Christian answer: "Thine is the kingdom and the power."

A Way of Understanding Our Changing World

In 1962 Thomas Kuhn developed a concept of paradigm change to explain the historical process of scientific development and progress.[3] He also indicated that the same concept can be used to understand social adaptation.

A paradigm is a world view based upon assumptions about reality and perceptions about the nature of things. It exists where people are committed to the same rules and standards and have a consensus about reality. As we try to make sense out of our experience in the world, we form our paradigm of the way things are. However, when our assumptions, beliefs, and theories are tested and proved to be wrong or inadequate, we develop or accept new ways of understanding and our paradigm changes. A paradigm change can be painful, because it involves the death of cherished theories and attitudes and the birth of new ones. As a result, such change is usually resisted strongly.

For those who believe that Jesus Christ is the Son of God, his advent, his life, teaching, death, and resurrection mark the greatest paradigm reversal the world has ever known. Some of those most directly affected by it resisted to the point of crucifying the messenger. And to this day those who accept the Christian paradigm have difficulty communicating with those who don't. We see things from a different perspective, and there is a long process of adjustment which is still taking place. Lesslie Newbigin in his book *Honest Religion for Secular Man* points out that "the New Testament has its own account of man's coming of age. 'During our minority,' says Saint Paul, 'we were slaves to the elemental spirits of the universe, but when the term was completed, God sent his own Son, born of a woman, born under the law, to purchase freedom for the subjects of the law, in order that we might attain the status of sons' [Gal.4:3–5]. This adult status is an invitation to responsible living as sons and daughters of the Father in whose hands all created things and all history lie. It is an invitation to deal boldly and confidently with the created world and all its powers. It is a deliverance from pagan fear of the mysterious powers of the cosmos. It is a desacralizing of the natural world which sets man free to investigate, and experiment and to control."[4] This outlook provided a foundation for modern science and technology which in due course produced the scientific age and the secular society in which we now live.

Christians are inclined to take a negative view of secularism, as being responsible for the decline of religious faith. However, Leslie Newbigin points out that the process of secularization now sweeping the world may well be a necessary stage towards a greater unity among mankind, and an eventual unity of spirit under the one God of the universe. People around the world today are for the first time seeing themselves as sharing a common history, facing a common atomic danger, and holding a common hope for a better world. I believe that in the due course of history, a united secular world will discover that it holds the most basic values in common, and that the purpose of the Creator for his world is that all people should live together in a caring cooperative community, locally and worldwide. In the meantime, those who accept the Christian paradigm have the responsibility of participating intentionally and creatively in the process of transition towards the goal of the kingdom of God on earth. Clearly, to be a Christian today is much more than minding your own business and trying to lead a good life. We have a mandate to be change-agents for God. At the meeting of the World Council of Churches in Vancouver in 1983, Archbishop Edward Scott said, "The Christian cannot rest until the values of the city of God have become values of the city of man."

Questions for Personal Reflection or Group Discussion

1 How do you feel about the "powerful forces which are revolutionizing our lives?" Do you feel like a powerless victim, or is there something you can do?
2 As you reflect upon your own life and faith, what are some of the major lessons you have learned and the key values you have adopted?
3 What do you think Jesus meant when he taught us to pray that God's kingdom would come on earth as it is in heaven?
4 Do you agree that we live in the overlap between the kingdom of God and the kingdom of man, and that a serious gap has developed between church life and the secular world?
5 What are some of the ways you can respond to the gap?
6 What do you think are the main causes of the "captivity" of the churches today?
7 What is our challenge and mandate as Christians in this age of transition?

2
The Unshakable Kingdom

Jesus came into Galilee proclaiming the Gospel of God: "The time has come; the kingdom of God is upon you; repent and believe the Gospel." Mark 1:14

Seek first his kingdom and his righteousness and all these things will be given to you as well. Matthew 6:33

The kingdom of God is not a matter of talk but of power. Corinthians 4:20

The kingdom we are given is unshakable. Hebrews 12:28

Catching the Vision

People prefer to give themselves to the things they consider most important. If serving God and his kingdom in our daily lives is not a priority with us, it is most likely because we have never caught a vision of the kingdom of God. If my religion is only about my personal salvation, so that I am, as the song puts it, "safe in the arms of Jesus," than maybe it is not worth any more of my time than keeping up the bare essentials: church going, financial support, personal prayer and study — paying my dues on the heavenly insurance policy, while I get on with the real business of living. In this case my God is too small and I have not caught the cosmic significance of my faith and the coming of Jesus Christ into the world. It probably means that I won't maintain the bare essentials for long either. Recently published figures indicate that in Canada church attendance has dropped from sixty per cent of the population in 1957 to thirty-two per cent in 1985. A decline of fifty per cent in twenty-eight years!

Unless we can visualize something we can't relate to it or make it happen. So before we get into the direct application of Christian values in management and business in later chapters, we need to take time to clarify the concept of the kingdom of God. Christian values in business are the values of the kingdom, as Jesus saw it in his everyday experience.

In Jesus we see the relationship between the kingdom of God and the kingdom of man. He knew that we have to pay taxes, and that the state has legitimate claims on us. Jesus lived in Herod's kingdom and in the Roman empire, but he also lived in God's kingdom. He manifested a special quality of life based on a different set of values. He calls us to follow his way.

If we study the lives of the men and women who have made a permanent impact for good on the world, we find that many of them had some kind of kingdom vision. Twenty years ago Martin Luther King wrote from his Birmingham prison, "Just as the eighth-century prophets left their villages and carried their 'thus saith the Lord' far beyond the boundaries of their home town, and just as the apostle Paul left his little village of Tarsus and carried the gospel of Jesus Christ to practically every hamlet and city of the Graeco-Roman world, I too am compelled to carry the gospel of freedom beyond my particular home town." Some called him an extremist. After his initial disappointment, he said, "I gradually gained a bit of satisfaction from being considered an extremist. Was not Jesus an extremist in love? 'Love your enemies, bless them that curse you. Pray for them that despitefully use you.' . . . the question is not whether we will be extremist, but what kind of extremist we will be. Will we be extremists for hate or will we be extremists for love? Will we be extremists for the preservation of injustice, or will we be extremists for the cause of justice?"[1] Martin Luther King's message was heard because it was embodied in his own life.

When any of us stand up to speak, it is as if there were an invisible screen behind us upon which the shape of our concept of the kingdom of God is projected. That is why it is so important for us to have a clear image of the kingdom of God.

What Is the Kingdom?

One of the reasons why we hear so little about the kingdom in church is that the biblical picture is not clear. The kingdom is a very complex idea which involves the total message of the Bible. It includes God's purpose for his world and man's place in it.

The problem is that although the kingdom was the dominant theme in the teaching of Jesus, he never defined what he meant by it. He gave many illustrations and visual images of the kingdom but he never provided a blueprint which we could follow. One reason is that a blueprint would soon have become outdated as civilization developed. But an image suggests a perspective on life and a way of looking at reality that continue to carry impact. Jesus said that "the kingdom of God is like" the pearl, the treasure, the son who returns home, the feeding of the hungry, the clothing of the naked, the visiting of the sick and imprisoned, the release of those in bondage. No technical definition could so powerfully portray for any people of any age such a kingdom of love, caring, and justice. It includes the concepts of wholeness, prosperity and abundance, physical health and security, and the free growth of the soul, in relationship to others in harmonious community. Thus Jesus has given us guidelines and clues and an open-ended vision which respects the freedom and creativity of his followers. In each age people like Augustine, Thomas Aquinas, John Calvin, Luther, and the modern theologians have wrestled with the meaning of the kingdom for their time.

Another reason why Jesus did not define the kingdom is that the Jews to whom he was speaking already had an understanding of it. The hope of the kingdom was a part of their everyday lives and they lived in anticipation of its coming. Central to this hope was the coming of the Messiah. This was only gradually made known in the Old Testament. So if we are to understand the concept of the kingdom, we have to begin with the Old Testament revelation.

The Kingdom of God in the Old Testament
The concept of God as king of the universe is very ancient and seems to be instinctive in man's attitude toward the Creator. It is a recurring theme in the psalms: "God is king of all earth; God

reigns over the nations'' (Ps 47:7). ''Declare among the nations, 'The Lord is King, he has fixed the earth firm, immovable; he will judge the people justly' '' (Ps 96:10).

For the people of Israel the formative event in history which constituted them as the people of God was the exodus. God's leading the descendents of Abraham out of Egypt, through the Red Sea to Mount Sinai where he entered into a covenant with them, is the most momentous event of the Old Testament. From their understanding of this event the Israelites recognized that God acts in history and is in control of it. The Ten Commandments made it clear that they had a duty first to God and then their fellow men. Thus they had a responsibility for the development of a culture which was based upon these two components. They, as the people of God, were to manifest the kingdom of God in their own community, but, as indicated in the psalms quoted above, God's reign has universal application. They believed that the activity of God as king provided the inner meaning of the universe.

The history of the Israelites is the story of their success and failure in keeping the covenant and manifesting the kingdom of God. They found it difficult to function without an earthly king who would represent the divine kingship on earth, so God granted them their request. Of all their kings, David came closest to the ideal, and their memory of his reign produced the hope that one day a king would rise in the line of David to establish an eternal kingdom. After David the prophets proclaimed the judgement of God on Israel because it had broken its covenant with him. The prophets also made it clear that hope for the kingdom was not confined to the nation of Israel. God would one day make a new covenant that would extend over the whole earth and include all people who turn to God. This led to the expectation that the Messiah would be a conquering king who would restore Israel as a leading nation of the world. The Israelites overlooked the prophetic message that God would accomplish his mission through a Messiah who would be a suffering servant, and that through his self-offering on the cross the eternal kingdom would be established.[2]

A final component of the Old Testament understanding of the kingdom of God is the apocalyptic hope, found mainly in the book of Daniel. It is believed that God will finally intervene at the end of history and establish his kingdom over the whole world. He will do what man has been unable to do, because ultimately the kingdom is not man's but God's.

Jesus and the Kingdom

Because Jesus was born into this climate of expectation among the faithful, the kingdom of God is the central theme of his teaching, and shapes his understanding of his own person and work. He made it clear that he was concerned with nothing less than the renewal of the world on the lines of God's original purpose.

The Problem of Evil

We cannot understand the life and teaching of Jesus unless we come to terms with the reality of evil in the world. It is probably the greatest of all theological problems, and one which is subtly avoided in most Christian circles. The subject is distasteful. We have the uneasy feeling that somehow we are all involved in the world's evil, and our guilt prompts us to maintain a conspiracy of silence, as we recoil from the daily news of mass murders, torture of innocent victims, economic exploitation, and oppression.

There is a cosmic battle between good and evil which is constantly being waged behind the scenes and which erupts onto the stage of the world and into the daily news. I have been helped to face this reality by two writers. William Stringfellow is a New York attorney and theologian whose book *An Ethic for Christians and Other Aliens in a Strange Land*[3] pulls back the curtain to reveal some harsh realities about the nature and extent of evil in our society. The other is Dr. Scott Peck, a prominent psychiatrist, whose own spiritual journey led him to write the best seller *The Road Less Travelled* in which he brilliantly integrates traditional psychological and spiritual insights of evil.

Dr. Peck writes, "I have come to conclude that evil is real. It is not the figment of the imagination of a primitive religious mind feebly attempting to explain the unknown. There really are people, and institutions made up of people, who respond with hatred in the presence of goodness and would destroy the good insofar as it is in their power to do so . . . . Evil people hate the light because it reveals themselves to themselves. They hate goodness because it reveals their badness; they hate love because it reveals their laziness . . . . I define evil, then, as the exercise of political power — that is, the imposition of one's will upon others by overt or covert coercion — in order to avoid extending oneself for the purpose of nurturing spiritual growth. Ordinary laziness is nonlove, evil is antilove. [4]

Dr. Peck enlarges on this understanding of evil in *People of the Lie* in which he writes: "Evil is in opposition to life, it is that which opposes the life force. It has, in short to do with killing . . . . Evil, then, for the moment, is that force, residing either inside or outside of human beings, that seeks to kill life or liveliness. And goodness is its opposite. Goodness is that which promotes life and liveliness."[5]

While I was writing this book, the contrast between the forces of good and evil was being vividly portrayed in the news. In Beirut a group of Shiite Muslim terrorists were holding hostage forty Americans on TWA Flight 847; one American serviceman had already been shot and killed. Air India flight number 182 with 329 people on board was blasted out of the sky at 30,000 feet over the Atlantic as it approached the coast of Ireland. The East Indian community in Toronto was in shock at the tragic loss of family and friends.

At the time Mother Teresa of Calcutta was visiting Toronto to open another convent for her order, the Missionaries of Charity. She was seen moving among the bereaved families bringing comfort and in a public address she prayed for all concerned and asked for a spirit of forgiveness for the terrorists. She said the worst thing in human experience was not hunger or suffering but being unwanted and unloved, having no one to care. Her life has been given to providing such caring love to the unloved. Two forces in the world, one taking life and the other giving life!

Of Satan, the very spirit of evil, Jesus said, "He was a murderer from the beginning." Evil has nothing to do with natural death; it is concerned with murder of the body or spirit. If our adversary the satanic power, who is by nature "the father of lies"[6] can masquerade as an "angel of light"[7] and convince us that he does not exist, then we will become complacent and spiritually lazy, a condition fatal to the Christian life.

Jesus began his ministry by confronting this evil power in the wilderness. Here he wrestled with who he was, and the what and how of his mission. He had several options, most of which would have been a fatal misuse of his power.

For centuries the Jews had been ground under the heel of foreign domination, and they looked for a Messiah who would deliver them from this bondage. In both Judaism and the early church, Satan was believed to be the real power behind the kingdoms of this world. Jesus did not dispute the power of Satan when he "showed him all the kingdoms of the world in their glory. 'All these,' he said, 'I will give you, if you will fall down and do me homage.' But Jesus said, 'Begone Satan! Scripture says, "You shall do homage to the Lord your God and worship him alone." ' "[8]

As we reflect upon world history and the tyrannical rule of kings and dictators, the Adolph Hitlers and Idi Amins, we are forced to recognize the real power of death that is still given to earthly rulers who pay homage to the powers of darkness. The cosmic battle continues, and we are faced with the same choices. Are we captives of the kingdom of man, or are we freedom fighters for the kingdom of God? Jesus felt so strongly about the tension his followers would experience in living in two worlds that in his farewell prayer for his followers he prayed to his heavenly Father, "I do not ask you to take them out of the world, but I do ask you to keep them safe from the evil one."[9]

Jesus' Vision of the Kingdom

The New Testament scholar C.H. Dodd indicates that in the ministry of Jesus the sovereign power of God was operating. In his actions we are witnessing the "powers of the world to come" and it is in this light that we must understand Jesus' teaching about the kingdom. Jesus saw his task as the establishment of a new covenant between God and a new Israel.[10] He was inaugurating a new kingdom to fulfil the task which the old Israel had failed to accomplish.

Jesus saw the kingdom of God as a developing process with small beginnings. He said,

> How shall we picture the kingdom of God, or by what parable shall we describe it? It is like a mustard seed, which is smaller than any seed in the ground at its sowing. But once sown, it springs up and grows taller than any other plant, and forms branches so large that the birds can settle in its shade.[11]

Jesus also saw his ministry as a sowing time rather than as the harvest time. He knew that the message, the seed, would fall on various types of soil. But there is a natural, God-given process of growth at work, over which we have little control. It is God's kingdom, not ours, and it will develop in his way.

Because of its slow natural growth, the manifestation of the kingdom would not be spectacular. When Jesus answered the Pharisee's question, "'When will the kingdom of God come?' He said, 'You cannot tell by observation when the kingdom of God comes. There will be no saying, "Look, here it is!" or "there it is!"; for in fact the kingdom of God is within you.'"[12]

This belief is strengthened by Saint John's gospel, in which it is recognized that the kingdom of God is a matter of inner spiritual perception. Jesus said, "In truth, in very truth I tell you, unless a man has been born over again he cannot see the kingdom of God"[13] and, "whoever does not accept the kingdom of God like a child will never enter it."[14]

Nevertheless Jesus did not repudiate the inherited Jewish concepts of the kingdom. He used Isaiah 61 as the opening text for his ministry and to declare his vision for humankind. "He has sent me to announce good news to the poor, to proclaim release for prisoners and recovery of sight for the blind; to let the broken victims go free. . . . "[15] But Jesus' concept or vision was of the inner kingdom in the reborn nature of humankind. His kingdom represented the most radical paradigm change in history: the power of vunerable love, servant leadership, the poor and humble entering the kingdom more readily than the rich and powerful and the high achievers, and the idea that a man's life does not consist in the abundance of his possessions.[16]

These concepts have seldom been taken seriously by the followers of Jesus, yet I believe that the world is only just beginning to discover not only that Jesus' way is to be taken seriously, but also that it is the only way we can function satisfactorily on earth. For example, many of the more enlightened managers of the most successful companies are beginning, in their dealings with people, to follow management practices which are in tune with many of the teachings of Jesus.

Jesus and his followers looked forward to the coming of the kingdom in its fullness, but what actually came at Pentecost was the church, the fellowship of believers in Jesus as Lord. The invisible kingdom in the hearts of men and women began to take visible form in the Christian community. The responsibility for the management and development of the kingdom was passed to the church.

Ideally the church should be a model of God's kingdom in the midst of the kingdoms of the world, and each congregation should be an outpost of the kingdom, a "colony of heaven" on earth. However, it is dangerous to equate the church with the kingdom. The church is God's primary agent or instrument of the kingdom in the world, but taken together, the churches are a rather mixed bag with diverse teachings and sometimes conflicting values. The church is sometimes disobedient to her Lord, and sometimes conforms to the world and its values and loses its capacity to witness to the kingdom. In other words the kingdom of God is much bigger than the church. It remains an ideal, but it is an ideal which our Lord expects us to strive for, and in proportion to our obedience and faith he will, through his Holy Spirit, supply the power we need, "for the kingdom of God does not consist in talk but in power." The kingdom and the power are of God.

Christianity and Culture

As time went by, the early church was forced to defer its expectations of the imminent return of Christ. It settled down to work out the implications of the concepts of the kingdom of God for the political and economic realities of life. In other words, it began to relate Christianity to culture.

In our society we tend to think of culture in a rather narrow sense. Cultured people are thought of as those who have good taste in music and the arts. Actually it is a very broad and inclusive concept. Culture is the social heritage of a people, the sum of all the ways and means by which a people understand themselves as individuals, their life together, and the institutions through which they express these understandings. Culture is a human achievement and includes language, education, philosophy, government, law, beliefs, art, science, and technology. Because these activities are designed to serve the good of humankind, our culture is an expression of our values. Humans shape their culture until it has an independent reality of its own, and then it shapes us, as we become "cultured." So culture is both the incarnation of our corporate spirit and the environment in which our consciousness is formed.

Culture is the day-to-day context in which the kingdom of God overlaps or conflicts with the kingdom of man. Robert Webber sums up this interaction: "The activity of the Christian in culture should be to unfold God's creation according to the purposes of God, so that every area of culture reflects Christian values."[17] This ideal is a lot easier said than done. Christians live in the world, the realm of culture with all of the responsibilities that involves supporting our family and working in a competitive business environment. But we are also called to live in the realm of the kingdom of God, which is based on a different value system. "In Christ we are called to selfless love, to servanthood, but in the world mankind operates largely out of selfish interest motivated not by service but by gain . . . . No matter how good a person may attempt to be, he is still caught to one extent or another in the corruption of a system that creates and perpetuates evil. And so the Christian is always trapped in that tension between what he is called to be in Christ and what he can actually become in the world."[18] This is the problem of the Christian in culture, and it must be resolved both personally and as a Christian community.

The problem has been resolved in a number of different ways in the course of history, and Richard Niebuhr in his book *Christ and Culture* identifies five different major responses to the problem.[19]

1 Some have seen Christ as being *against* culture, and these have tried to separate themselves from the influence of the wicked world.

2 Some have seen Christ as the *fulfilment* of their own culture and society. They select and accommodate his teaching to fit their own views.
3 Others see Christ as *above* culture because they believe that the basic issue is not between Christ and society, but between God and humankind.
4 Some recognize the paradox of the authority of Christ and culture *in tension*, and call Christians to live in the tension until it is resolved beyond history.
5 This view sees Christ as the *transformer* of culture.

Christ the Transformer of Culture

In my view, this approach to the problem of how to live within the two realms simultaneously is the most practical and helpful way to follow. It is significantly different from the approaches which advocate separation from culture or identification with culture. The major difference is the conviction that culture can be converted and changed. The most noted exponents of the transformational approach have been Augustine in his *City of God*, John Calvin, and F.D. Maurice. It is also the perspective from which this book is written.

The transformers have a positive and hopeful attitude towards culture. Richard Niebuhr points out that this positive view is based on three theological convictions. First, on creation theology, which emphasizes the ongoing creative activity of God in the world in and through human beings made in his image. The creative Spirit of Christ continues to work in the lives of his people as they give practical expression to their belief in the incarnation of Jesus and his work of atonement and redemption.

The second conviction emphasizes the nature of humankind's fall from created goodness. This fall is the result of human rebellion, which in turn has led to the corruption of culture and the distortion of our values and actions. The solution lies in the transformation of society by the application of kingdom values and perspectives.

The third conviction is based on a view of history as the story of God's actions and our responses to them. The focus is on the presence of God in time, and eternal life is understood as a quality of life which begins in the here and now and continues beyond death. There is less concern for past traditions or a final future; the concern is with the "divine possibility of present renewal . . . ."[20]

The English theologian F.D. Maurice powerfully expresses the transformation view of the kingdom, "The kingdom of God begins within, but it is to manifest itself without. . . . It is to penetrate the feelings, habits, thoughts, words, acts, of him who is the subject of it. At last it is to penetrate our whole social existence. The kingdom of God is transformed culture, because it is first of all the conversion of the human spirit from faithlessness and self-service to the knowledge and service of God."[21]

The Kingdom in the Workplace

Christian action applies to all areas of life; however, our particular concern in this book is upon the role and responsibilities of Christians in the workplace. Before we can deal with any confidence with the particulars of our mandate for action in the workplace, it is essential that we have some clear biblical terms of reference.

The book of Genesis is one of the most remarkable in the Bible. As the name implies, it is a book about the beginning of things: the beginning of creation, the beginning of the human race, and God's purpose and plan for life on earth. God's instruction to the first man and woman, "Be fruitful and multiply, replenish the earth and subdue it: and have dominion . . . over every living thing that moveth upon the earth"[22] is the cultural mandate given to humankind. It is God's purpose for life on earth. We are made in the image and likeness of God in order to have dominion over the earth, to continue the creative process, and to be responsible stewards or managers of the resources of the earth. When we do this we manifest the image of God.

Throughout the Bible the primary emphasis is not upon some otherworldly spiritual existence, but upon the development of human culture on earth. The Old Testament provides detailed instructions for the people of God regarding their politics and economics, their family and work life. And in the New Testament Saint Paul has much to say about the integration of faith and work; he makes no distinction between physical and spiritual work, they are both serving God. "The new person, restored in Christ, is to work in God's world to supply the needs of others, to shape the development of human life."[23] Saint Paul's attitude to work was in marked contrast to the attitudes of the other cultures, which viewed work as fit only for slaves. He regarded all aspects of life and work as equally religious when done in service to God. This perspective on work may provide the clue to the kinds of attitudes and values we will need in the future, in which employment or work for pay may only be available to a minority of the population. In other words, if as a reflection of the image of God we engage in constructive activity, a basic human need may be satisfied without a direct relationship to income, which could be received on some other basis, such as nationally guaranteed annual income.

We are called to use our different gifts and to exercise our cultural mandate, but as a continuing result of the Fall, our greed and pride tend to corrupt human affairs, and we live with a mixture of good and evil in society: great beauty, creativity, and loving actions mixed with scandal and oppression. This realistic view of human nature reminds us that while we work towards the kingdom of God on earth, we can expect disappointments and setbacks. We do not expect to achieve Utopia, but we do believe that change and improvement are possible with the exercise of responsible stewardship and loving relationships. We are to be in partnership with the God who promises to make all things new, and gives meaning, purpose, hope, and excitement to life.

James Taylor in his book *Two Worlds in One* states that "The real problem about living in God's kingdom is learning to hear God, not just on special occasions, but on an everyday basis. . . . I really believe that most people today are more familiar with God's absence than God's presence; they know God second hand, through the Bible or through their minister's sermons but they do not, themselves, have much sense of daily and continuing contact with God."[24] Saying yes to God is relatively easy. Living in the kingdom is hard. It means living daily, as if God is in charge, when reality may appear otherwise. This is what it means to "seek first" his kingdom.

Our Terms of Reference

To sum up, let me suggest the Christian's terms of reference for action in the workplace.

1. Our mandate as the people of God, made in his image, is to continue the work he has given us as co-creators with him and as stewards of the earth's resources for the good of all people. We are to be witnesses to the love of God in Christ, who came to restore the broken relationship between humankind and God.
2. The basic problem we face is the fact of evil both personal and corporate, originating in the satanic power which holds sway behind the scenes of our history, the continuing negative effects of the Fall and its corrupting influence on society, the reality of human sin, and our tendency to prefer to do things our way rather than to obey God.
3. "The Bible is the story of how sin has been, is being, and will be overcome through Jesus Christ. It is the story of how mankind has been and will be redeemed and restored to fellowship with God."[25] That story points us to the ultimate victory, when the ideal for which our Lord taught us to pray, "Thy kingdom come," shall be realized.

Questions for Personal Reflection or Group Discussion

1. What does it mean to you to be living in the overlap between the kingdom of man and the kingdom of God? What does being a member of the kingdom of God mean to you?
2. What are some of the main elements of Jesus' vision of the kingdom of God?
3. How seriously do you feel Jesus expects his followers to take his prayer that God's kingdom would come on earth?
4. Is the problem of evil a reality which you take seriously? How do you explain evil in the world? What is the Christian response to the power of evil?

5 Discuss the relevance of the five ways in which Christians have related the gospel to culture, as identified by Richard Niebuhr. What has been your experience in this regard?
6 Discuss our mandate for Christian action in the workplace and our terms of reference.

3
The Power of Values

Several clues indicate that the industrial world may be experiencing the beginning phase of a socio-cultural revolution as profound and pervasive in its effects upon all segments of society as the Industrial Revolution, the Reformation and the Fall of Rome. Willis Harmon

A Society without a Purpose

In this era of Star Wars and robotics, the very survival of our advanced human civilization is dependent upon our developing an intelligent understanding and practice of values. Values guide the choices we make about such critical issues as the development, deployment, and use of our technology. Without them, we lack the criteria for effective decision making and our society becomes a ship without a rudder. Because we are in an age of transition, there is in our society a confusion and a lack of consensus about values, which makes government and business decision making extremely difficult.

This lack represents the major challenge to the church in our time, and the domain of values is now the major arena for significant lay ministry. Pronouncements within church circles will not have much effect upon the world, but the laity in business, industry, and government can be effective agents for change for God — provided they have a clear vision of the values of the kingdom of God and know how to translate these values into policy and action.

Unfortunately in business, we have substituted a largely mechanistic philosophy for spiritual and human values. The end justifies the means, and the end is the economic bottom line. This value system leads us to put property rights above human rights, technological development above human development, and competition and adversarial relationships above co-operation. Thus, for example, when business has to decide whether or not to replace employees with robots, the human factor is seldom taken seriously, and the decision is based on the more easily quantifiable economic values such as efficiency, productivity, and profit.

Our political system, like our economic system, is not expected to be a source of values; it is expected to facilitate the achievement of the desired ends of individual citizens according to their particular value systems. But the fact that our society is made up of a plurality of cultures makes it very difficult to achieve a consensus. When we add the fact that in recent years many values and attitudes have changed radically, it is not surprising that we now have a value-confused society. We have a system of economic means and a system of political means but we have no unified system for defining the ends for which these means exist.

In the past, Christian culture was the integrating force for Western civilization. Our modern society, by separating the spiritual dimension from the rest of life, has largely removed this dimension from our cultural consciousness. "The world-transforming attitude of Western man remains, to be sure, but as it is increasingly deprived of its ultimate religious justification, it becomes uncertain, unstable, progressively empty of moral content . . . . If human beings no longer know what purpose their lives should have, even the most marvelous technological and economic achievements become implausible — and, in the end, not worth the effort. Democracy itself, arguably the most noble fruit of Western history, becomes mere procedure and bereft of moral authority"[1]

The practical application of Christianity and the ministry of the laity involves the intentional re-integration of spiritual and human values in the day-to-day decisions of life and work. This requires the healing of the divorce between science and religion, which began in the eighteenth century when it was believed that science and its application in technology would eliminate the need for belief in God. The re-marriage is based on the recognition that science is simply the discovery and application of the laws of nature which were instituted by the Creator.

The need is urgent, because in our fast changing world "we have not, as a society, identified a set of social values to guide us in a deliberating way into the future."[2]

The questions we face are, Do we as human beings have a moral responsibility to choose the shape of our future on this planet, or do we just let the future happen and hope for the best? And if we do choose to control our future, upon what values do we base our actions? The thesis of this book is that although Christianity does not provide the detailed blueprint for the future, the life and teaching of Jesus Christ provide the basic values and guidelines upon which a global society of love, justice, and peace can be built.

A New Language

I believe that values and value-based concepts are the keys to the re-integration of theology and real life. Values may be defined as *the criteria we use to make our choices and decisions.*

One of the most exciting and far-reaching implications of learning how to move from theological concepts to values is that it immediately opens up the possibility of a universally acceptable and understood language. Most of the time, theological language is neither appropriate nor understood in the business world, but values are a part of everyday life and work in all cultures.

Theology shapes Christian values and those values form our images of success, goodness, attractiveness, etc. Our value-based images are then the basis of our choices and decisions which constitute our lifestyle or workstyle. This process may be visualized as follows.

Theology 〉 Values 〉 Images 〉 Lifestyle/Workstyle Choices and Decisions

Neither Christianity nor any of the other world religions has a monopoly on sound values. There is a growing number of people who are concerned about the fate of the earth, about ethical and moral principles, who do not share a religious perspective but with whom we can work towards common goals. If we wait for theological unity, before we work co-operatively, the world may not survive. We can go a long way towards a co-operative future by discovering our common values.

The Hierarchy of Values

It is important to recognize that all values are not of equal importance; there is a hierarchy. God represents the supreme value, the supreme worth; all the other values flow from the central value, from the core spiritual values down to the need-based or pragmatic values. The variety and the options increase as we move down the scale of importance, and this gives richness and individuality to our lives. My preference for blue over green is a value choice, but it is of little importance compared to the choice of justice over exploitive profit, or personal growth over status. We develop norms of behaviour at the various value levels. This can lead to confusion, because at the inconsequential level it may be all right to settle for situation ethics, in which circumstances determine the moral choice. At that level there may be no right or wrong, only difference and preference and these don't really matter.

However, as we move up the scale of values they matter increasingly, until we reach the kind of ultimate values for which people are prepared to fight and if need be to die. These are the ultimate spiritual norms which derive from the knowledge of God revealed in scripture.

The Value Revolution

John F. Kavanaugh, a Jesuit priest and associate professor of philosophy at St. Louis University, in his book *Following Christ in a Consumer Society* provides a penetrating analysis of what is happening to us under the pressure of the prevailing value system which is *thing* centred rather than *person* centred. He identifies two competing gospels in our society. They are radically different and they serve as ultimate and competing forms of perception through which we filter all of our experience and understand ourselves and our world. These competing world views are the *Personal Form* and the *Commodity Form*. The personal form of gospel reveals persons as irreplaceable and uniquely free beings; the commodity form of gospel reveals men and women as replaceable and marketable commodities. (This is another way of expressing the competing cultures of the kingdom of God and the kingdom of the world as described in Chapter 2.)

> The pre-eminent values within the Commodity Form of life are marketability and consumption. These two values are the ethical lenses through which we are conditioned to preceive our worth and importance. They have profoundly affected not only our self-understanding but also our modelling of human behaviour (into manipulation and agression), human knowledge (into quantification, observation, and measurement), and human affectivity (into noncommitalness and mechanized sexuality).[3]

This means that in many families love must be earned or proved, and education is valued exclusively in terms of grades. And we speak of "job markets." In our society marketability is king, and the unspoken question is, Will I sell? If you are not part of the productive system, you are considered useless and worthless, whether you are one of the economically poor or the unproductive elderly.

What this means, in effect, is that there is no intrinsic human uniqueness, worth, or value. Friendship, love, happiness, and joy become commodified in products to be bought; our worth is related to our appearance, possession, and accomplishment. Our "freedom to choose" is mainly between more products and scenarios for success. We live in fear of becoming redundant or obsolescent — no longer useful to the system and permanently unemployed. The power of evil hardly needs to bother with the peccadillos that some preachers are inclined to rail against when, by the subtle process of secularization, humans are transformed into commodities who have ceased to experience the reality of the spiritual dimension. The spiritual death and dehumanization, which are the objectives of evil, will have been achieved.

Fortunately that scenario is only a partial reality. The other side of the picture is the growing number of the followers of Jesus in all denominations who are taking their membership in the kingdom of God seriously, and are ready to move from a reactive to a pro-active Christian lifestyle. They are ready to move from the commodity form to the personal form. Also the church is emerging from its cocoon, to take a more active part in the political and economic struggles of the poor and powerless of the world, and in shaping the future.

In 1976 when the economy was booming, George Cabot Lodge identified a trend in the United States away from the traditional Adam Smith ideology, which emphasizes individualism, property rights, competition, the limited state, and scientific specialization, towards a new ideology, which emphasizes communitarianism, the rights and duties of membership, community need, the active planning state, and interdependence. Simply put, he felt that we were moving from the *me* generation to the *we* generation. Many of the underlying values in the new ideology were much closer to the kind of co-operative community values of a Christian ideology than the traditional approach.

In 1979 I conducted a survey of business managers to determine the extent to which this trend could be identified in Canada.[4] In answer to the question, Does the Canadian business community have a clear and effective ideology? the response was negative. A majority of sixty per cent said, "No, but we should have one"; nineteen per cent said, "No, and we don't need one"; and twenty per cent felt that we do have a traditional ideology. But it is significant that sixty per cent recognized a need for a unifying ideology and were presumably prepared to move in this direction.

There was a considerable difference in the value perspectives of the older senior excutives and the younger managers. The older managers (over 50 years) were committed to the traditional Adam Smith values, whereas the younger managers were more open to the humanitarian values. The communitarian aspect of the emerging ideology defines what is good and right from the perspective of the whole society, rather than that of individuals and corporations, for example, pollution control and energy conservation. The majority of respondents felt that the new ideology is influencing the Canadian business operation; however, there is clearly a tug of war between the traditional Adam Smith ideology and the new.

It is important to clarify what I believe is a Christian position on the issue. Sometimes those who are critical of the competitive individualism of our system are automatically labelled as communists or at least as socialists. From this perspective there appear to be only the two extremes, either individualism or collectivism, and if you are against one you must be for the other. From a Christian point of view both extremes lead to injustice and oppression. Individualism is the leading of one's life without regard for others. This is the philosophy of the me generation which could lead to anarchy and chaos. Its corporate expression is unrestricted free enterprise. The other extreme, collectivism, tends to subordinate the rights of the individual to the needs of the state, which results in the loss of personal freedom and oppression.

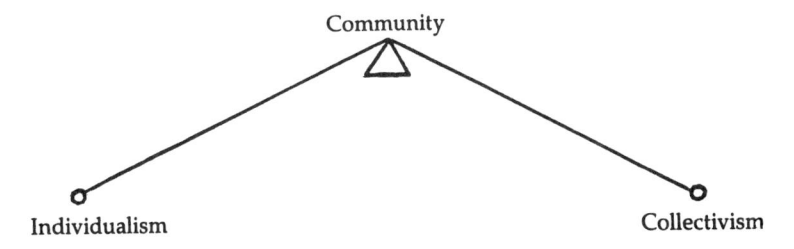

```
                    Community
                        △
                       ╱ ╲
                      ╱   ╲
                     ╱     ╲
                    ╱       ╲
                   ○         ○
            Individualism    Collectivism
```

Both extremes are distortions of genuine needs, and the integration of the two concepts in a balanced form is what Christian community is all about. Jesus taught the supreme value of the individual; he also formed a community, beginning with the basic unit of the small group of twelve disciples. He taught the philosophy of love and service to others to the point of self-sacrifice. To love God and your neighbour as yourself sums up his ideology. It has been said that Christian conversion is in many ways a conversion from individualism, independence, and alienation to community. It is community which holds in balance the need for individual freedom and respect, and the need for voluntary self-discipline and restraint for the good of the whole group or society.

The Performance Gap

Our reason for being involves personal growth and the struggle to achieve "mature personhood, measured by nothing less than the full stature of Christ."[5]

We all fall short of this ideal and it is helpful to distinguish between our ideal and our operative values. We may quite sincerely profess to believe in the ideal biblical values; however, our operative values are those by which we actually make our choices and decisions in life. They determine how we use our time, energy, and money.

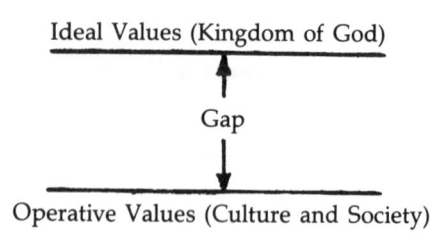

```
        Ideal Values (Kingdom of God)
        ─────────────────────────────
                      ↑
                     Gap
                      ↓
        ─────────────────────────────
        Operative Values (Culture and Society)
```

Most of us are painfully aware that we fall short of the ideal, but our recognition of the gap and our efforts to close it are what our personal growth and spiritual development is about. If the gap between our profession and our practice is too great, our integrity will be in question and our faith may not survive. For example, we may idealize love and yet not be loving people, for we learn to be loving, not simply by hearing about it in church but by being loved and loving in return.

Struggling with the gap is where the personal battle of faith takes place in our work situation. This is where the crunch is felt by those who are forced to compromise their personal values and ethical standards by the pressures of business. This is where we discover the depth of our commitment to the values of the kingdom of God. It is where we need the moral support and prayers of a group of fellow Christians who understand and can provide counsel and encouragement, so that we can find the grace and strength to live what we profess to believe.

For example, the struggle for power in one form or another is at the heart of most individual and corporate conflicts. How does a Christian value power differently? Generally in our society, power over an individual is valued as a means of domination or control, whereas for the Christian, power is valued as a basis for service, to help others develop their gifts and strengths. It requires courage to be different, but as Saint John wrote, "My children, love must not be a matter of words or talk: it must be genuine, and show itself in action."[6]

The way we make our choices is the key to the application of our faith in daily life and work. An authentic Christian lifestyle involves making choices which are true to both who we are and what we believe and value. There are of course some things about which we have no choice, but most of the things that really matter are determined by our own choice. Our behaviour is the result of our choosing and deciding. If I treat my employees or fellow workers with love, dignity, and respect, it is because I have chosen to act that way. If I act like a slave driver at work, it is because I have chosen to live by a different set of values. Accepting responsibility is the price of freedom, and many people are afraid of freedom; they would rather be told what to do, or hide behind company policy and petty rules, rather than take responsibility for a difficult moral choice. Suppose a good employee has missed a number of work days because his wife has been ill, but it is company policy to terminate employment for absenteeism. Do you simply follow the rules or do you try to work out an alternative that will save the man's job?

Our personal growth and development are largely determined by our willingness to take risks and to take responsibility for our own choices. This is why Jesus used a teaching style which did not give direct answers to questions; he responded with deeper questions which forced the seeker to answer and choose for himself. "People experience freedom when they perceive alternative courses of action open to them and have some kind of value system on which to choose between them."[7]

We are putting our faith into action when we make responsible choices between what is important and what is not, and choose the essential, the valuable, the true, the honest, the just, the good, and the excellent. Viktor Frankl points out that "when fundamental decisions have been made, when a course has been chosen that keeps one's life open to God and thus to the ultimate values in life, then a sense of quiet and contentment fills the heart."[8]

A Value-Based Vision

Because "business is the dominant social group in America with the greatest influence on social values,"[9] the ministry of the laity in the business community is one of the most strategically important areas of Christian ministry today. It is the real mission field of the nineteen-eighties and beyond. It is the most effective way the values of Christ, entrusted to the Christian community, can get outside the church and into the world. I believe that once they learn how to be intentional about their religious beliefs, managers, lawyers, investors, engineers, teachers, and politicians — the decision makers — can powerfully influence the values of our society. For the past nine years, men and women associated with the King-Bay Chaplaincy have been learning how to do this.

The first challenge is to develop an awareness of the relevance and power of spiritual values in the workplace. The church itself does not appear to be fully aware of how directly the gospel applies in this environment; yet Jesus spent most of his time in the marketplace, in the fields, by the lakeshore with the fishermen and the business people of his time. His stories and parables were designed to teach the values of the kingdom as they applied in everyday life and work. We are called to continue that ministry.

I used to think that to follow the teachings of Jesus in the modern world, and particularly in the business world, would be a prescription for economic suicide. The jungle warfare of the competitive business environment was no place to practice compassion or to put people before profit.

However, during the past nine years of ministry in the business community, I have made several discoveries which have changed my mind. First of all, I discovered that many writers and leaders in the field of organizational and management theory are either operating from a Christian perspective or at least subscribe to spiritual and person-centred values. For example, many of the best-selling management books in recent years, such as *In Search of Excellence* by Peters and Waterman, make it clear that the value system of the executive leadership of corporations is the most important determining factor in building the kind of spirit in the organization which spells success. The Japanese industrialists attribute much of their success to the highly motivating "superordinate" values which provide a unifying and guiding force in their corporations. The founder of Matsushita Electric, one of the largest companies in the world, says that the secret is to harness the spiritual energies of the employees. He adopted a code of seven spiritual values, most of which are in harmony with those of our Judaeo-Christian tradition. Some people claim that the Japanese way of managing was related to their culture and would not work for us. This is not the case, as has been shown by studies of the corporate cultures based on clear values and beliefs. "The companies that did best over the long haul were those that believed in something."[10]

Thomas Watson Jr., the founder of IBM, built that organization on Christian principles and said, "I firmly believe that any organization, in order to survive and achieve success, must have a sound set of beliefs on which it premises all its policies and actions. Next, I believe that the most important single factor in corporate success is faithful adherence to those beliefs."[11]

In 1981 the McKinsey Company, a management consulting firm, published a report on its study of thirty successful Canadian companies. It found that most of these companies operated on values similar to those of the Japanese. They were highly people oriented, they really cared about their employees and their development, and they existed to provide a service. The report also indicated that the values held by the senior management seemed to pervade the whole organization and provided the dynamic which resulted in excellence.

In other words, many of the values of the kingdom of God, although not recognized as such, are being rediscovered by a pragmatic business community. I believe that an enlightened Christian laity could transform our society and move it from the philosophy of competitive individualism, the Adam Smith approach, to co-operative community, the Jesus approach.

A Practical Philosophy

My experience with Operation Bootstrap in the past three years convinces me that implementing these ideals in the workplace is a practical possibility. This program for unemployed business and professional people was developed on the basis of the following stated philosophy:

1. We believe that the pioneering value of people helping people is the most effective way to transform despair into hope and to get Canada working again.
2. We believe that co-operative community is a more effective way to function than competitive individualism, both in the business sector and society at large.
3. We believe that the whole person, body, mind, and spirit, must be cared for and developed in order to achieve health, happiness, and fulfilment.
4. We believe that effective living requires the balanced integration of personal, family, work, and recreational needs in relation to one's fundamental values.
5. We believe that all people need the support of a trusting, caring, and affirming community, which can develop quickly if people reach out to each other.
6. We believe in the creative potential of the individual and that this is our greatest resource for building a better future.

Operation Bootstrap is not a religious program in the traditional sense, because it is open to anyone who needs it. We do not use religious language, but when people have an opportunity to rethink their values and the meaning and purpose of their lives in the context of a caring and supportive community, they are not far from the kingdom; and for many, it is a deeply spiritual experience. The results have been inspiring. Depression, despair, and a loss of self-worth have been transformed into hope, confidence, and the creativity that has started a host of new businesses. Over a thousand men and women have been helped to return to work.

We witnessed new life as these people became a caring and enthusiastic community committed to helping each other. As I see it, these results are evidence that applied Christianity is a transforming power which could build a new society.

How does theological theory apply in a practical way in real life? How can Christianity apply to the workplace? For me, the answer came with the recognition that values provide the means of translating faith and theological concepts into everyday application, particularly in the workplace. I believe that theology is the way people make sense out of a sometimes confusing and difficult life experience. To that extent we are all theologians. We learn to think theologically when we have a clear concept of the nature of God and relate that understanding to our history and personal experience.

We move from "being" to "doing" in the light of some meaning or purpose, from identity to action through the power of choice based on our values. Whatever gives ultimate meaning and purpose to our lives is our god, and the kind of god we believe in is the major determining factor in our values and actions. If we believe God is just and merciful, we will value justice and mercy. If we believe God is vengeful and unmerciful, we will be inclined to seek revenge and demand our pound of flesh. From my personal perspective, a God who chooses to relate to a suffering world as the suffering servant, embodied in a caring community of love, makes more sense than any of the other concepts of God I have found.

When we learn how to extract the values from Jesus' teachings, I believe we will find that they are not only relevant but that he was indeed the way, the truth, and the life for all time.

The Christian World-View

I have attempted to develop a statement of a Christian ideology or world-view, based on the biblical revelation of the nature of God. It is bound to be somewhat subjective and it is not possible to do justice to many other valid points of view. However, it is worth the attempt. The following is offered as a useful frame of reference.

1. God is the sovereign Lord who creates and sustains the universe.
2. The created world is good and reflects the providence of God, who continues to be involved in the process of human history and in individual lives, through the operation of the Holy Spirit.
3. Humankind is made in the image of God and shares the capacity to love and create, to communicate and relate. As a result we have the capacity to rise to great heights of love, beauty, truth, and creativity.

4 God's gift of free will and freedom of choice is misused by humankind to rebel against God and his will for us. This reveals the other side of human nature, which can descend to the depths of degradation, cruelty, and destruction. Therefore a Christian ideology takes the reality of human sin and corruptability seriously, and recognizes the need for forces to maintain law and order. It rejects utopian notions of human perfectability.
5 There is a cosmic struggle between good and evil. The power of evil is real and continues to influence human affairs. It is an anti-life force which deals in lies, deception, and death.
6 God has a plan for the world, based on his reign in human hearts and lives. The kingdom of God on earth is a community of right relationships based on love, justice, and *shalom* — the peace of God.
7 The kingdom of God was inaugurated by Jesus Christ. In his life, teaching, death, and resurrection he bridged the gap between God and humankind. As the Servant-Lord, he desires the love and allegiance of the people of God, and in his life and teaching he modelled the lifestyle and values of the kingdom.
8 God's plan involves a partnership with humankind in the co-creation of the world and its future. This gives meaning and purpose to our lives. Human beings and their institutions are responsible as stewards and managers, accountable to God and the human community for the best use of the human and material resources of the earth.
9 Within the stewardship context, the function of business and industry is the provision of goods and services for human benefit in a manner that is economically viable, and provides a high quality of working life for its employees.
10 God's plan is not static, but is an unfolding process in which he relies upon us as co-creators to work out the details through the use of the gifts of mind and skill he has given us.
11 Human cultures reflect the value systems of those who create them and are derived from the kind of gods they worship. The kingdom hierarchy of values flows from our vision of God as the supreme value, and his revelation in scripture provides the basis for our norms and moral authority.

12 A Christian ideology affirms the primary and equal value of each human being, and is committed to individual freedom and growth within the context of a mutually responsible community. The concept of the primary value of the person provides a guide for the formulation of political, business, and economic goals and policies.

These norms represent ideals, but they are not impossible; they are indications of what Jesus meant when he taught us to pray that his kingdom would come on earth as it is in heaven.

Questions for Personal Reflection or Group Discussion

1 Do you agree that our society's values are confused and lack a sense of purpose? How does this relate to your own values and sense of purpose? Does your faith make a difference?
2 How do you respond to the statement that the ministry of the laity involves the re-integration of spiritual values in the day-to-day decisions of life and work?
3 Would the use of values language make it easier and more practical for you to express your faith in the workplace? In what ways?
4 Do you agree with John Kavanaugh's analysis that we are in a critical ideological struggle between the Commodity Form, or thing-centred culture, and the Personal Form, or person-centred culture? In what way does this help to clarify your mission or ministry?
5 In your company what is the potential for influential value-based leadership by Christians in management positions?
6 What practical guidelines for the workplace can you deduce from the Christian ideology or world view?
7 Try to visualize how your department, and then your company as a whole, would function if it operated on a basis of Christian values. What leverage can you apply to tilt the system in that direction?

4
Values in the Workplace

Many are acknowledging that the single most critical factor in increasing productivity today lies with the company itself in its approach to people. Peter Drucker

If we want to create high performance organizations that cause people to stretch and grow, to be happy, and to be extremely effective, we would do well to base them on spiritual principles. The kind of high energy found in the top-performing organizations is at core a spiritual phenomenon. James A. Ritscher

The Systems Age

Russell Ackoff, professor of systems science at the University of Pennsylvania, believes that "we have entered into a period which will be to the future what the Rennaisance was to the past. We have moved into a new age that is fundamentally different from the age from which we have come, and we are attempting to deal with problems generated by a new age with techniques and tools we have inherited from an old one. These are the dislocations of our culture."[1]

One of the major causes of the paradigm shift in our understanding of the way things function is the revolutionary shift from the machine age to the systems age. "During the Machine Age the world was conceived of as a machine, a machine operating is accordance with laws which are dictated by the structure of the world."[2] This led to reductionism, which is the process whereby everything is broken down into its constituent parts as a way of understanding its nature. The parts can then be put together like a machine. When Frederick Taylor applied this mechanistic view to organizations, they were seen as machines in which people were parts. Taylor was an engineer who used time and motion study of jobs to reduce physical work to its component parts, so that people could most efficiently be related to machines in the mass-production process.

This approach produced the age of the specialist for every part of the human anatomy, and each ailment is treated as a separate entity. But humans are not machines; they are whole persons. When they are physically hurt, depressed, or afraid the whole being is affected. A breakthrough in modern medicine is the holisitic approach to health which is concerned with the whole person. We know that full health requires the health of body, mind, and spirit. To be sick in any one of these areas affects our whole being.

The same breakthrough is taking place in all areas of life and work. This systems view of reality holds that the performance of the whole is affected by every one of its parts. Russell Ackoff describes it as the Systems Age.

This systems viewpoint reverses the mechanistic approach; you begin by understanding the nature and purpose of the whole system. Then in the light of that understanding you can discover the nature and purpose of the parts. The designers of the ill-fated Edsel car made the mistake of thinking that by taking the best features of many other cars and simply combining them in one model, they would have the supercar. It failed miserably because it was not an integrated whole, the parts were not designed in relation to the whole concept. The system is more than the simple sum of its parts, just as a person is more than the sum of his of her constituent parts. A physical examination does not determine the personality or the spirit of the person. Similarly the performance of the whole is not achieved by the addition of the performances of the parts. The art of management is the effective synthesis of the whole organizational system.

The heart of the systems approach is communication. The incredible advance in communication technology is radically transforming our society, and the information age is superseding the industrial age. We have reached the almost godlike stage in which, if we can imagine it, we can produce it. Computer-assisted design and computer-assisted manufacture are manifestations of this technology.

The machine extended man's capacity for physical work, now technology is assisting man's thinking processes. By combining electronic communication systems with instruments that can observe and record changing data (temperature, pressure, direction), a computer can generate new data such as course corrections for a space vehicle. This data-processing technology can now do some forms of man's mental work, and the next generation of computers will be thinking machines!

When this technology is combined with self-regulating machines, we have *cybernation*, a system that can regulate and adjust itself to changes in its environment and circumstances. But to what purpose will we apply this marvellous capacity? We have mastered the *means* and the *ends* are now limited only by our creative imagination. This has both frightening and exciting possibilities.

The key concept behind the systems age is *control* through *communication* in the light of *purpose* and *values*. This is the basis of the second Industrial Revolution.

We can draw an interesting parallel to the biblical concept of creation by the Word of God. "When all things began, the Word (the purposeful communication) already was. The Word dwelt with God, and what God was, the Word was. The Word, then was with God at the beginning, and through him all things came to be: no single thing was created without him."[3] Thus God *controls* the process of creation through his *communicating* Word, in the light of his *purpose*. "And God said, 'Let there be light' and there was light." Then the purpose was made clear, "God said, 'Let us make man in our image, after our likeness: and let them have dominion . . . over all the earth.'"[4] This *process theology* affirms that the universe is not a purposeless evolutionary machine but a *teleological* design originating from the ultimate purpose in the mind of God: that his kingdom should come on earth as it is in heaven.

Some of the trends in management philosophy identified in Chapter 3 have been influenced by a combination of changing values and systems thinking. I believe we are in a time of great opportunity, when it might be possible to transform and humanize business and industry on the basis of a new model. An organizational development model based on human characteristics and values rather than on mechanistic concepts would restore people and their values as the basic organizing principle of society; science and technology would assume the role of servants. I believe that this would be a step in the direction of the order of creation as God intends it to be. If we could combine this perspective with responsible stewardship under the sovereignty of God, the world system might then be in harmony with the kingdom of God.

The Human Being as Process Model

After exercising a ministry in the business community for a number of years, I realized that the research and writing I had done in the field of personal lifestyle development could readily be adapted to apply to the intentional management of an organization.

We get to know persons, first of all, by their observable behaviour. But we soon realize that their behaviour arises out of a complex system of commitments, values, and assumptions — their sense of who they are and what matters in life. If we want to relate to people in creative ways, we have to get to know them at a level which goes below the surface and takes seriously the complex dimensions of their personalities.

The same observations can be made about organizations. They have personalities and develop lifestyles. They cultivate a corporate image and act in certain ways which reflect their management style. They operate out of a complex system of motivations, values, and assumptions, many of which are never stated. Management literature now describes this as the *corporate culture*. When you join a company such as IBM you join a corporate culture, and if you want to be effective in the company, you have to learn the corporate values and standards.

Self-understanding and intentionality are essential to human growth and development. This is also true of organizations, and the same dynamic process can be applied to both. The basic principle of lifestyle formation is that we move from *being* to *doing*. We begin our lives with a process of identity formation, or the development of our inner being. Individually, we discover our self-identity by becoming aware of our own history, our values, beliefs, attitudes, and personality traits, which are integrated into our world-view. Then in the light of who we are, we exercise the power of choice and translate our inner self-awareness into external behaviour, relationships with others and actions in the world around us. We develop a sense of meaning and purpose in life. It is an interactive process: if my purpose is to become a Christian business person, then as that purpose is realized, being a Christian business person becomes part of my identity.

As we accept responsibility for our own growth, we develop an experimental attitude. We attempt to discover and express who we are and how we feel about ourselves and the world. We make choices and decisions which affect ourselves, others, and our world. The free exercise of choice and decision is the key to being intentional about the formation of our lifestyle. We can chose our friends and decide how we are going to relate to them. We can decide how we are going to organize our time, use our energy, and spend our money to achieve our purpose and goals in life.

This process of personal formation and growth can be expressed in a life-management model in which life is controlled through communication in the light of purpose and values.

Life-Management Model

Life-Management

Self-identity, life purpose, beliefs, and values

Information Flow — Control — Goals

Input	Transformation	Output
Personal traits: character, social environment, education, health, etc.	Decisions about: relationships, use of time, information, energy, and money	Personal lifestyle

Feedback

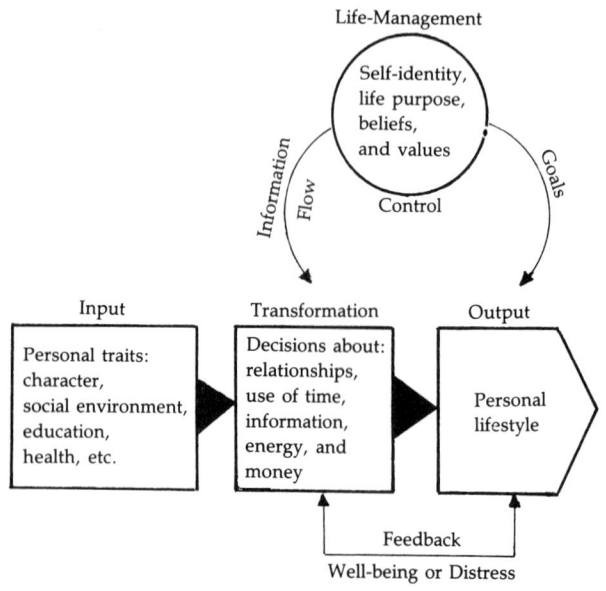

Well-being or Distress

This life-management model indicates that the key to an intentional and inner-directed lifestyle is the development of a clear sense of identity, purpose, belief, and values. If these are unclear or confused, the individual is likely to become a victim of circumstances and will be controlled by others.

The basic element of our life-management control or direction, as shown in the circle, is the spirit of the individual which, together with the mind, determines the behaviour or lifestyle. It is the basis of our performance in life. If the spirit is changed the whole life system is affected; if my values change from power and domination to love and service, my lifestyle will change correspondingly. History has been changed by this type of personal transformation in people like Saint Paul, William Wilberforce, and Martin Luther King.

This human model can be applied to organizations. The following industrial Input-Output model indicates how an organization can be viewed on the same basis as the human model. The system's performance is controlled by its purpose and values. This dynamic process model resembles a human or organic life-form more than the traditional organizational machine.

Industrial-Management Model

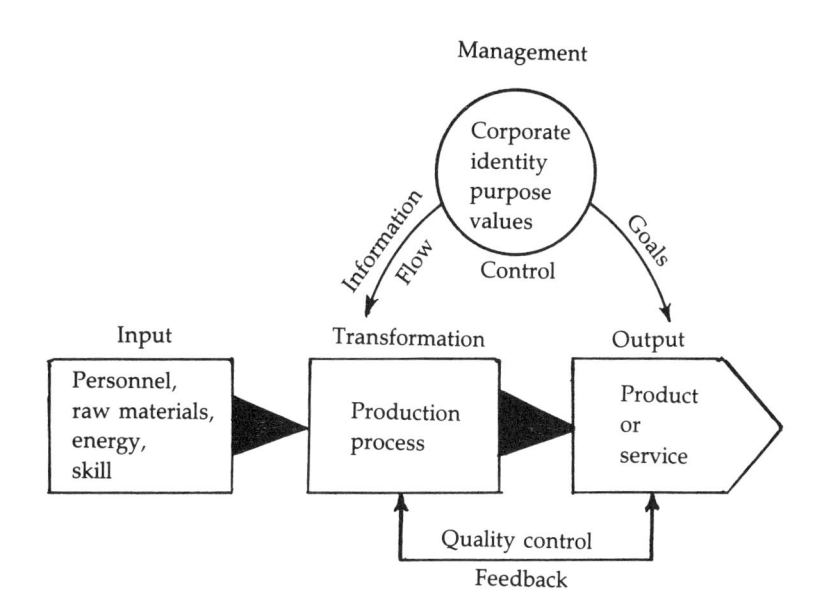

The key difference between the above process model and the mechanistic model is that people working in the systems process are recognized as having needs and goals of their own which can be integrated with the needs and goals of the organization. In the mechanistic model, the people in the organization were simply the means to the ends of the organization. In the process model the values and performance of an organization are affected by the changing values and attitudes of those who work in it. Management adapts the shape of the organization and its leadership style to reflect the creative capacity of people in a participative team. This is the basis of a new quality of working life and quality-control circles. Workers make decisions and develop their own job according to its particular purpose and the overall purpose of the organization. This approach reflects a Christian view of people who, made in the image of the creator God, exercise responsibility in a free but co-operative community.

The Systems Approach

One of the major implications of the systems approach is that the world is not static; we live in a process of continual change. But the rate of change has increased dramatically in our time. Systems thinking has become the only way we can cope with ongoing change. In a static world one could solve a problem and it would stay solved. But if variables such as the market, needs, and values keep changing, then information feedback becomes essential to adapting the system to changes and avoiding rapid obsolescence. Only those companies and organizations which can adapt will survive in the future.

Change is now occuring at such a pace that reacting to present experience alone does not give enough lead time for the organization to adapt in an effective manner. Research and development are essential in the systems age to enable the organization to develop a future perspective and anticipate and adapt to change.

Purposeful Organization

The second major implication of systems thinking is that organizations must be purposeful if they are to be effective. Purpose is the glue which holds the system together; it provides the basis for intentional management. The purpose may range from mere survival to creative service, but without it neither individuals nor organizations can survive.

The parts of a machine have no purpose in themselves other than to contribute to the purpose of the whole machine. When organizations were viewed in this way in the machine age, the people in the organization were treated as parts of the machine.

It is significant that coincident with the growth in organizational understanding, there has been a growth in individual self-awareness in our society, and a drive for greater self-determination by individuals. This development has created a major paradigm shift in the workplace and presents management with the complex problem of how to integrate the values of the employees with the purpose and values of the company. Personnel must be recognized as individuals who have their own needs and purposes and the desire to participate in the decisions which affect their work.

The ideal result of this radically new way of understanding organizations is to see them as co-operative human communities, organized in relation to a common overall productive purpose. They are communities within which the individual needs and purposes of the employees are taken seriously and, as far as possible, integrated with the life and purposes of the company.

This new understanding of organizations points to the possibility of a new work ethic which could replace the old Protestant work ethic which is no longer an effective motivator.

Robert Greenleaf, an active Christian and former director of management research for AT&T, proposed a new ethic which he stated as, "*work exists for the person as much as the person exists for the work.* Put another way, the business exists as much to provide meaningful work to the person as it exists to provide a product or service to the customer."[5] This does not mean the creation of inefficient make-work projects, but the improvement of the *quality of working life.* This is the title of a new philosophy and methodology in business and industry which is based on respect for the dignity and creative potential of the individual.

Ministry to the Spirit of Organizations

Ministry to the spirit of an organization, I believe, is an exciting new form of service open to lay people. Regardless of our position in an organization, we can have some influence on those with whom we work. Whether we work on the shop floor, in the secretarial pool, or in the president's office, we need to explore how we can influence the spirit of our organization.

We can use the analogy of the human being as a way of thinking about the life of an organization. The *body* of the organization is made up of the people in it, and the organizational structure is the skeleton which gives it form and shape.

The *mind* is the problem-solving, planning, and decision-making capacity of the organization.

The *spirit* is the intangible combination of values, attitudes, and norms; the culture of the organization which determines its character or corporate personality.

The gospel is about personal relationships, wholeness, and health. I believe that God is also concerned with institutional and organizational wholeness and health. Just as the human spirit influences the individual's health, so the health and effectiveness of an organization can be influenced by a change in the corporate spirit. When Christian lay people learn how to change the spirit of the place where they work, it could result in the practical application of many of the values of the kingdom of God.

I believe that many of the organizations in our society are spiritually sick. They do not even recognize that they have a spirit. They try to solve their productivity and financial problems by physical reorganization and efficiency methods, when the problem may be poor employee attitudes and morale due to the complete lack of spiritual dimension in their corporate life.

As Richard Pascale and Anthony Athos observe in their book *The Art of Japanese Management,*

> By an accident of history, we in the West have evolved a culture that separates man's spiritual life from his institutional life. This turn of events has had a far-reaching impact on modern Western organizations. Our companies freely lay claim to mind and muscle, but they are culturally discouraged from intruding upon our personal lives and deeper beliefs . . . . Splitting man into separate "personal" and "productive" beings makes somewhat artificial parts of what is the whole of the character. When we do so, our cultural heritage not only too strictly en-

forces this artificial dichotomization, but deprives us of two rather important ingredients for building employee commitment. First, companies are denied access to higher-order human values, which are among the best-known mechanisms for reconciling one's working life with one's inner life. Second, the firm itself is denied a meaning-making role in society, and thus pays excessive attention to instrumental values, such as profit, market share, and technological innovation.[6]

The real malaise in many of our troubled organizations today, those with deep-seated labour and production problems, is neither technical nor economic but spiritual. There is a lack of moral leadership and a breakdown of trust, and, without a moral leader, human relationships sour. As Richard C. Hodgson of the Business School at the University of Western Ontario points out:

> The moral leader is the "conscience" of a top management team. He perceives what his organization should be. He articulates the key human values that his organization represents. He reinforces the worth of what the members are doing, and must do, to operate the organization. He gives meaning and purpose to the self-discipline required to run the organization.
> It is the currently perceived absence of such leadership that has called the value of many organizations, and most managers into question in the public mind.[7]

Surely this represents an opportunity for business executives with Christian convictions to provide the kind of value-based leadership that is required.

In the documentary film *Miracle of Pittron*, Wayne Alderson, motivated by a Christian concern, achieved a dramatic turnaround in a near-bankrupt steel company which was paralyzed by a bitter labour-management dispute. As vice-president in charge of operations he demonstrated the powerful effect of moral leadership and transformed the spirit of the steel foundry by treating the workers with dignity and respect. There was an astonishing increase in production and improvement in morale. However, the executive leadership of most business enterprises prefers to remain largely invisible and shuns expressing publicly its positions on the vital issues that affect business and society.

The Power of Values

I have come to realize that knowing the values of people or organizations is vital to understanding them. If you know who has the power in an organization and what their values are, you have some indication of their probable behaviour and future direction.

It is commonly accepted that religious belief is a private matter, quite separate from political and business life and decision making. However, research indicates that there is a strong connection. It was discovered that "if we want to guess how members of Congress will vote, it will not help much to find out what denomination they belong to. But if we know exactly what kind of God they believe in, what values they hold, and just how religion shapes their view of their place in the world, then we can predict with considerable accuracy how they will vote on particular issues.... The evidence is strong that ties between religious world-view and political decision making are profound...."[8] Presumably this research would also apply to business decision making.

This information coupled with the data from my survey of management values indicates the powerful influence that the church could have in the business community, if Christians could become more intentional in their application of faith in the workplace. I found it surprising to discover that in our sample eighty-seven per cent were Christian: seventy-nine per cent Protestant, and eight per cent Roman Catholic. (Wallace Clement found a similar distribution in the United States business community.[9]) Our respondents were also above the national average in strength of their beliefs and extent of church involvement: forty-three per cent had strongly held beliefs and thirty-one per cent had moderately held beliefs; forty-eight per cent were active in their church life and worship and twenty-three per cent were occasional attenders. Ninety per cent of the church people indicated that their beliefs were relevant to their work situation. However, the majority, sixty-six per cent, felt that beliefs are a private matter, and thus presumably apply their faith in a personal way in the workplace: in personal honesty, and in caring personal relationships. Only thirty-four per cent saw their faith as having public or corporate application. This is clearly the result of the gap which has developed between the church and the world. The potential for influential leadership by Christians in management positions is very great. God may not be on the agenda of the board and senior management meetings, but spiritually based values could be, if managers had the training and courage to be intentional about their faith.

It may be helpful at this point to reflect on the term *spiritual values* because it can have a wide range of meanings. For some people it would mean specifically Christian values, and would have a rather narrow application within the Christian community. However, it is interesting to note that there are relatively few uniquely Christian values; most are held in common with Judaism and other world religions. Our theological rationale for holding the values may differ, but the basic values, such as truth, honesty, justice, and the value of human life are widely held. Spiritual values reflect the highest aspiration of humanity from a moral and ethical perspective. Although Christian people strive to live by the values of the kingdom of God as revealed by Jesus, Christians can find much common ground for co-operative action with those of other theological beliefs. I am sure most Christians would have no difficulty agreeing with the sentiments expressed by Konosuke Matsushita, founder of Matsushita Electric Company. In his book *Not for Bread Alone*, he expresses the philosophy upon which he has built one of the world's great business organizations.

> We do not live by bread alone; however, possessing material comforts in no way guarantees happiness. Only spiritual wealth can bring true happiness. If that is true, should business be concerned only with the material aspect of life and leave the care of the human spirit to religion and ethics? I do not think so. Businessmen, too, should be able to share in creating a society that is spiritually rich and materially affluent.[10] (Business competition should be) based not on power, but on something with more lasting value. . . . I am talking about a moral code, an ethic, that provides a standard for right and wrong. Such a code should dictate how we conduct our activities, for without it, society would become the domain of the

powerful, determined only by those with brute strength on their side. The rule of power does not bring prosperity: quite the contrary, history has shown time and again that power, unchecked, leads to violence.[11]

Many companies in our North American society could benefit from this Japanese value-perspective.

Servant Leadership

There is obviously a need for leadership, but the question is, What kind of leadership is appropriate and effective in our kind of world? Michael Maccoby in his book, *The Gamesman: Winning and Losing the Career Game*, describes four typical leadership styles: (1) the Jungle Fighter, who will do almost anything to look good; (2) the Craftsman, who takes pride in his work; (3) the Gamesman, who thrives on a fast-paced, competitive game; and (4) the Company Man, who is concerned about the long-range value of the institution.[12] There is no one perfect style of leadership and different styles seem to be appropriate under different circumstances. Our concern is to find a style that is particularly appropriate from a Christian perspective and to see how it might fit the modern management environment.

The basis for power and authority is changing. Property and ownership have traditionally provided the right to manage, but increasingly in our society the right to manage is given by those who are managed.

According to management consultant Robert Greenleaf,

> A new moral principle is emerging which holds that the only authority deserving one's allegiance is that which is freely and knowingly granted by the led to the leader in response to, and in proportion to, the clearly evident servant stature of the leader . . . . To the extent that this principle prevails in the future, the only viable institutions will be those that are predominantly servant led.[13]

As an active Christian, Robert Greenleaf no doubt was influenced by Jesus' teaching on servant leadership. He gave us our model when, although he was aware of his infinite power, he chose to wash his disciple's feet. It is a strange paradox that greatness comes from exercising humility. This does not mean that we pretend to be less than we really are. It is simply a matter of recognizing that all we have and are comes from God, and that our strengths and abilities are gifts to be used in his service. The kingdom and its power are of this nature. Leadership that empowers others may appear to be based on weakness, yet it is the kind of power that moves the world in the long run. It elicits the kind of allegience which millions have given to the Christ throughout history.

The retired Episcopal bishop of Atlanta, Bennet J. Sims, has established an Institute for Servant Leadership under the auspices of Emory University's Candler School of Theology. The program of the Institute is based on the work of Robert Greenleaf, and it is attracting business executives to its week-long seminars and follow-up weekends. In Canada the prestigious Niagara Institute and Centre for Leadership Development attracts senior decision makers from business, labour, and government to its programs on Human Values in Organizational Life and Leadership and Vision.

Some of the characteristics of servant leadership identified by Greenleaf are:

1 An unusual openness to inspiration. The essence of leadership is going out ahead to show the way. The inspired leader sees farther ahead than his peers. Where such vision is lacking, leaders tend to try to preserve the existing system.
2 Not much happens without a dream. The true leader has a visionary concept and an overarching purpose.
3 The servant-leader has a great capacity for listening.
4 The servant-leader always empathizes, always accepts the person but sometimes refuses to accept the person's effort or performance as good enough.
5 The servant-leader has a highly developed left hemisphere of the brain for logical thinking, but also a highly developed right hemisphere which enables him to see things whole and with an intuitive foresight, a feel for patterns and the ability to generalize beyond limited data.

6 The leader is able to think of *now* as the moving concept in which past, present moment, and future are one organic unity. This is the basis of foresight.
7 The servant-leader has a keen awareness and perception. He can tolerate a sustained wide span of awareness so that he can see things as they are. He has an inner serenity that can cope with the stress produced by wide awareness and perception.
8 Leaders need the gift of persuasion, in order to acheive change without coercion.
9 The servant-leader knows who he is and is determined to be his own person.
10 One of the most important leadership talents is the ability to conceptualize, to translate dreams into concepts which can be put into concrete action.

These servant-leader qualities are required for the participative style of management which will be characteristic of the creative and flexible organization in the future. Participative management incorporates a team approach which involves various levels of management in the decision-making process. This improves the quality of the decisions and assures more widespread understanding and implementation of the decisions made. This trend points to the growing awareness of the importance of building a sense of community in the organization.

Change Agents

It is easy to feel overwhelmed and powerless in the face of world events. Feeling that there is nothing we can do to effect change, we tend to retreat into a pietistic religious stance, concerned only with individual personal salvation. Meanwhile the "principalities and powers" of evil continue largely unchallenged as they oppress and dehumanize people around the world. Christians have traditionally believed that the way to change the world for God is to change the individuals in it. I believe it is more effective, if, in addition to helping individuals change, we learn how to change the organizations which tend to shape the life and values of both individuals and society.

An exciting example of the power and effectiveness of Christian values in the workplace is Service Master Industries. This company was the most profitable among the top-rated five hundred service-oriented companies over the last ten years. Its return on stockholders' equity averaged 30.1 per cent. Significantly, the company was built and continues to operate on Christian principles and values. Its basic philosophy is summed up in four principles: to honour God in all we do, to help people develop, to pursue excellence, to grow profitably. Mr. Kenneth T. Wessner, chairman of the board, explained these principles as follows.

1 To honour God in all we do
"Our company recognizes God's sovereignty in all areas of our business. Our objective is to apply consistently the principles, standards, and values of the Bible in our business attitudes and actions.

2 To help people develop
"Our company believes that people grow with the challenge and opportunity for achievement that requires an individual to stretch. Employess will be encouraged to expand their abilities and potential through the company's educational and training programs and education outside of the company. In recruiting, developing, and training employess, the company will provide an equal opportunity for all.

3 To pursue exellence
"Our company accepts the responsibility continually to seek better methods to render current and new services to its customers at better value. Our trademarks and service marks stand for excellence. We are committed to continue serving each of our customers with a pursuit of excellence.

4 To grow profitably
"Our company sees growth in revenue while maintaining an adequate profit both as the material means of achieving the other purposes and as a measurement of the company's values to its customers, employees, and shareholders. Our company is com-

mitted to use profit with a sense of stewardship and responsibility to employees and customers while providing a means for profitable investing. We are also determined to share these benefits of the free enterprise system domestically and throughout the world."[14]

What more challenging and exciting Christian ministry could there be than for lay people to learn how to function as effective ambassadors of the kingdom of God, based on a practical vision of the way things should be and could be in their particular work place.

Questions for Personal Reflection or Group Discussion

1. Do you feel that computers, robots, and technology are threatening and have a negative effect upon human life, or do you celebrate these developments as products of our God-given creativity? Discuss how you think Christians should respond.
2. Can you see any implications for the message of the kingdom of God in the key statement of the Systems Age, "Control through communication in the light of purpose and values"?
3. Discuss ways in which the management model of input and output on page 00 can be used to understand and develop the lifestyle of both the individual and the corporation.
4. Discuss the implications of Robert Greenleaf's proposed new work ethic, "work exists for the person as much as the person exists for the work."
5. Do you agree that learning how to minister to the spirit of your organization is one of the most important aspects of the ministry of the laity in the workplace? Discuss how you would exercise this ministry in your company.
6. Do you agree that our society is suffering a crisis in morale largely due to the lack of moral leadership? In what ways could business executives provide such leadership and how could the local church encourage and support it?
7. Do you agree that the servant leadership style as described in this chapter is a Christ-like model which is not only practical

in modern organizations but the style most likely to result in *shalom* in the workplace?

8 Use the list of characteristics of servant leadership identified by Robert Greenleaf on pages 00 as a basis for self-examination and meditation. If Jesus were chief executive officer of your company, do you think he would function this way?

5
Value-Based Management

Value-based management is a process which uses the unifying and motivating power of key values to develop the human potential in an organization. It fosters a co-operative team spirit which increases organizational effectiveness and productivity. Management Support Systems

Value Conflicts

Canada's record of work days lost through strikes and absenteeism is one of the worst in the Western world. I believe that one of the root causes of this industrial disease is unresolved value conflicts between labour and management.

Most of the time our values operate below the surface of our consciousness, and because other people are not aware of these motivating values they may misinterpret our behaviour. This is the source of a great deal of human misunderstanding and conflict, both personal and corporate. Unfortunately, value conflicts cannot be solved by rational argument, because each side is reasoning from a premise the other does not understand.

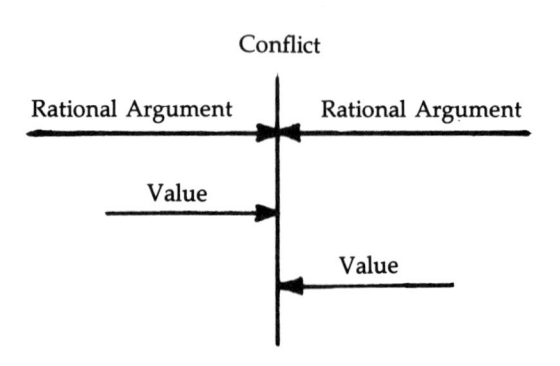

For example, if two people with different socio-cultural family backgrounds get married, they may find that they frequently get into irrational arguments over behaviour they find irritating in each other. One assumes that the other person is either stupid or stubborn not to see the obvious good sense of the opposing point of view. Different upbringing has led to a clash of values below the surface of communication. Unless the two people find a way to deal with it, their communication problem may end in divorce.

If, on the other hand, there is some sensitivity to the nature of the problem, and sufficient love and trust for each to risk vulnerability, then the problem can be resolved. For example, a wife might say to her husband, "Jack, I am proud of my farming background and way of life, and when you say things that put down that lifestyle, it offends my values." A new level of understanding and changes in the behaviour can result. Imagine what might happen if the Russian and American peace negotiators began their sessions by comparing the basic values of the Russian and American people, instead of arguing over a win-lose power game.

If there is considerable difference in the workplace between the values of management and those of the other employees, there is likely to be constant conflict and misunderstanding. If teamwork is the key to a successful operation, then some way of increasing the degree of mutual value awareness could make the difference between survival and excellence.

Some management consultants tested this theory with rather startling results. They identified what they considered to be ten typical work-motivation values. They distributed the list to both the managers and the managed, and asked each to rank the items in the order of greatest importance. The following diagram vividly contrasts the different value perspectives of the two groups. The potential for labour-management conflict is obvious.

70 *The Faith-Work Connection*

Motivation to Work
Contrasting Work Values

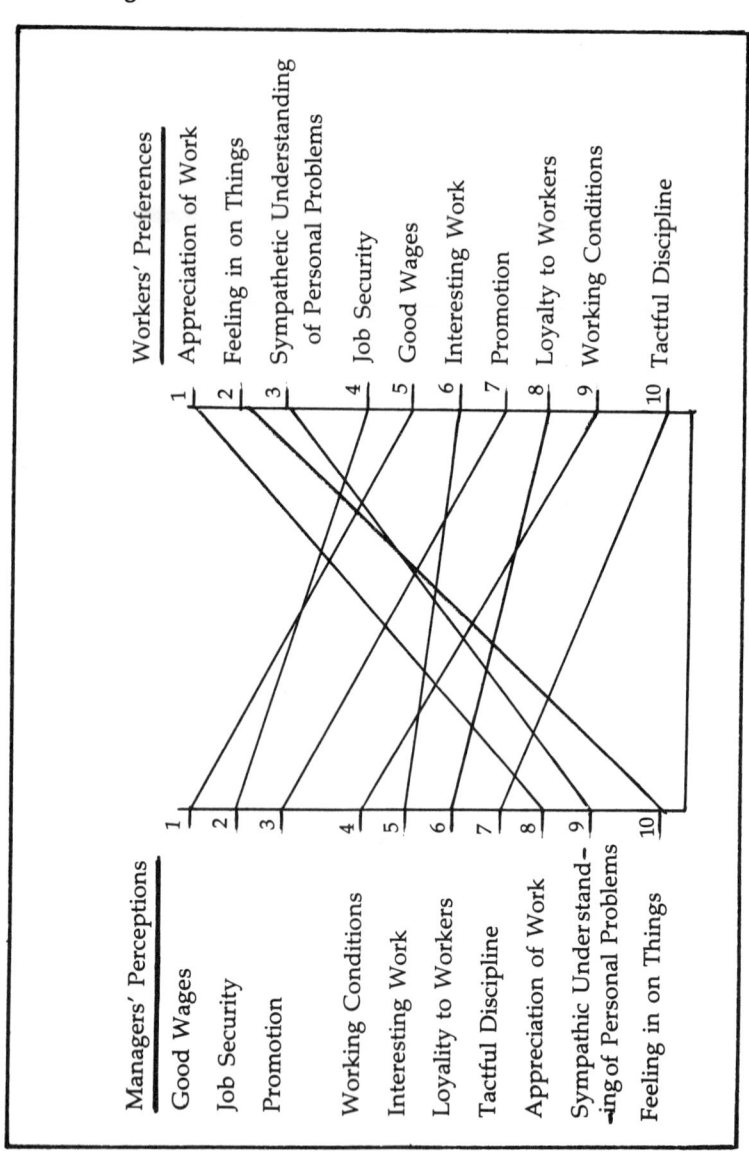

Managers' Perceptions		Workers' Preferences
1 Good Wages		1 Appreciation of Work
2 Job Security		2 Feeling in on Things
3 Promotion		3 Sympathetic Understanding of Personal Problems
4 Working Conditions		4 Job Security
5 Interesting Work		5 Good Wages
6 Loyality to Workers		6 Interesting Work
7 Tactful Discipline		7 Promotion
8 Appreciation of Work		8 Loyalty to Workers
9 Sympathic Understanding of Personal Problems		9 Working Conditions
10 Feeling in on Things		10 Tactful Discipline

Contract negotiations between management and union representatives become a long and hostile process when each side tries to achieve by rational argument a set of widely divergent goals based on different values. Unions only become necessary when the corporate philosophy endorses exploitation of the workforce. Matters which are justly due to employees are grudgingly given as concessions and have to be wrung from a reluctant management by a show of union power.

If the real issue at the bargaining table is the need for workers to be treated with the dignity and respect of mature adults and the company is treating them as hired hands or units of production, the issue is based on values and will not be solved by heated arguments over wages. If the only common language the negotiators know is money, the battle may be fought on the wrong ground. Even if the financial demands of the union are met, the underlying issue has not been dealt with and the we-they adversarial relationship will continue to destroy the company spirit and undermine productivity.

The solution is to change the relationship from that of distrustful adversaries to co-operative partners in production. This requires sufficient mutual trust to be able to communicate at the values level. However, it takes time and risk to build trust, and management may have to change its philosophy regarding openness and disclosure of financial information to employees. The witholding of information is a sure way to create suspicion and distrust; the second item on the workers' list of values was the desire to feel in on things.

Value-Based Management

As a means of relating to the business community in a businesslike manner, the King-Bay Chaplaincy established a small subsidiary organization called Management Support Systems. This is a group of Christian business people who are interested in the practical application of spiritual values to develop organizational health and effectiveness. Over a period of a few years we developed the concept of value-based management and a framework for its application. The idea was to develop an approach to organizational health and effectiveness based on an integration of spiritual values and a sound approach to organizational development and management.

1 Value-based management (VBM) is a way of managing an organization based on an understanding of the values which motivate the company and its people. It is a style of management which is flexible enough to adapt to rapidly changing needs and new technology.
2 VBM requires a strong sense of corporate identity and purpose to inspire employee commitment to the goals of the organization.
3 VBM achieves the purpose and goals of the company by creating a strong corporate community and team spirit, based on mutual trust, shared values, and open direct communication.
4 VBM integrates the values and personal goals of the people in the organization with the values and goals of the company, to achieve their creative and productive potential.

A Management Model

In order to achieve organizational health, it is necessary to have some way of considering the whole corporate body as an interrelated system. The following diagram is the way we visualize the essential elements of an organization.

A Dynamic Management Model

The model is based on the following ten elements of management:

1 Corporate purpose or mission
2 Corporate sense of identity
3 Management philosophy and culture
4 Corporate sense of community
5 Management leadership style
6 Organizational structure
7 Human resourcing
8 Labour-management relations
9 Technological development and utilization
10 The operational systems.

Because these elements represent key areas of management concern in a dynamic organization, it is critically important to subject them to a value analysis to determine the health of the organization and to provide a basis for strategic planning.

The Spirit of the Organization

Using the analogy developed in the previous chapter we see the human organization as a combination of body, mind, and spirit. Our model is designed with the three elements that shape and develop the spirit in the centre, the elements of corporate purpose, identity, and philosophy. These are the primary executive responsibilities and provide the overall sense of direction for the company. The influence of the spirit permeates the whole organization. Lee Iacocca succeeded in the dramatic turnaround of the Chrysler Corporation by creating a new spirit dedicated to "being the best."

The corporate spirit, expressed in appropriate leadership styles, shapes the strategy for the development of the company and its business. If the corporate spirit is healthy it will reflect shared values and an enlightened approach to human resourcing and labour-management relations. Techological development will be handled in a manner which integrates advanced technology with human or social considerations. All of this then results in the operational system, the way we do things in this company. This includes the policies and procedures used to co-ordinate activities to achieve the objectives of the company.

The whole system is held together by the outer circle in the model, the sense of corporate community.

Corporate Purpose or Mission

Research has shown that the most successful companies recognize the power of a corporate vision: a clear and compelling sense of purpose which provides a sense of direction and inspiration throughout the organization. There is a close relationship between a company's purpose and its identity. Most organizations begin with a purpose which, to some extent, shapes their sense of identity. Then in time the identity may reshape the purpose. The scope of the purpose is critically important, because if it is too narrow, it can quickly become irrelevant in a rapidly changing society. Purpose defines the direction and motivation of the system; it provides a reason for belonging to or working for the organization. Purpose may be externally imposed by the owners or shareholders, or it may be internally generated by management.

The purpose of the organization for which we work is naturally a primary concern for a Christian. A high-performance organization dedicated to excellence must itself become a positive spiritual force in the world. It will have a vision of doing what is good, not only for the stockholders but also for its employees and for society as a whole. One of the most energizing qualities of spirituality is a sense of purpose in life, a vision of something larger than the individual. The vision and purpose of an organization represent its spiritual quest, and when the employees are able to identify with that corporate purpose, they are committed and energized.

As we reflect upon our company's purpose we need to ask, Is it committed to excellence? Does it exist primarily to serve society? Does it also exist for the benefit of its employees? Does it inspire loyalty and commitment to the organization? Does it serve genuine needs, and what kind of impact is the product or service having upon society?

Corporate Identity

The image and sense of identity of an organization has a direct influence on employee morale, loyalty, and *esprit de corps*. People tend to live up to their "name," and to have a good name in a community influences the behaviour of an entire family. So it is with an organization; the name and image are closely connected with the intangible but all-important company spirit.

The corporate image can be either positive or negative. A business friend of mine worked as an engineer for a company which, as a result of its pollution record, had a bad public image. The company had supplied him with a briefcase with the company name and logo on it, but he was so ashamed of being associated with that company, that he removed the identification from his briefcase and eventually left the company. On the other hand, a corporate spirit of excellence provides the employees with a moral compass which affects the quality and productivity of the organization and sets its standards of performance and behaviour.

Identity is formed, first of all, out of a sense of origins or roots. Most companies have a variety of ways of telling their story to themselves and the community. (The church uses its liturgy for this purpose.) Usually the image of the organization is a reflection of the values of its founder, but as the company grows and leadership changes, the spirit of the organization may change and the original dynamic may be lost.

When I began my ministry with the King-Bay Chaplaincy, a business friend who worked for a large investment firm showed me around the establishment, with its sophisticated computer technology and instant global communication system. Jim had been with the company since it started, and he commented on how things had changed. He said, "In those early days, working for this company was like being part of a big family. Old Charlie, the boss, knew everyone by name and you felt as if he was interested in you as a person. But now it's so big and impersonal; there is a different spirit in the company."

It seems that the key to maintaining a particular corporate image and spirit is to institutionalize the values of the founders. IBM has largely been able to maintain the values of Thomas J. Watson Jr. by emphasizing service and the personal growth and development of the employees. Similarly, William Hewlett and David Packard, founders of the multinational Hewlett-Packard electronics company, have been able to maintain a dynamic corporate identity since first publishing their objectives in 1957. These objectives are constantly updated and well publicized. Corporate health requires that senior management focus continuing and intentional attention on the corporate identity.

As Christians we have a responsibility to help build a positive corporate self-image or identity. It would be useful to ask such questions as, Is the organization's name widely known by the public? Is it associated with excellence in our line of business? Is the average employee loyal to the company and proud to be associated with it? Is the company highly regarded as a corporate citizen, with a reputation for quality and a concern for people and the environment? If the identity of the company is based on widely shared values, the employees can identify with it and feel empowered by it. Empowerment is essentially a spiritual concept, but of course a Christian uses power for service, not self-aggrandizement or domination. Servant leadership is based on giving power to others, and is effective because empowered individuals create a dynamic organization.

Corporate Philosophy and Culture

William Ouchi, author of the book *Theory Z* which combines the best of Japanese and American management theory, states,

> A philosophy clearly sets forth the company's motivating spirit for all to understand. Whether directly or indirectly, that philosophy determines how insiders and outsiders alike appraise, trust, and value the organization and its products. . . . A philosophy can help an organization to maintain its sense of uniqueness by stating explicity what is and isn't important. It also offers efficiency in planning and co-ordination between people who share in this common culture. But more than a vague notion of company right-and-wrong, there needs to be a carefully thought-out philosophy, perferably one available to all employees in booklet form.[1]

The corporate philosophy clearly indicates both the means and the ends of the organization, its purposes and goals, and the way it will operate to achieve those ends. From a Christian point of view, corporate philosophy is the most important of the ten elements of management, because it is central to the company spirit and is the natural place to begin a prayerful reflection on the quality of life in your organization. Here the values of the world and the values of the kingdom of God meet. Gaps between the ideal and the actual can be identified and personal priorities and plans sorted out.

In order to maintain corporate health it is necessary to have a periodic audit of the company's operating philosophy and values. This audit identifies changing values and inconsistencies in profession and practice, and demonstrates to all employees that the philosophy and values are taken seriously by senior management.

(See Appendices 2 and 3 for an example of a corporate statement by Magna Corporation which reflects the spirit of the organization.)

The following questions may help you to reflect on the corporate philosophy and culture of your organization.

1. Does the company have a published statement of its management philosophy and values?
2. Is the statement a formality, or is it used consistently as a basis for policy and decision making?
3. Does it mean anything to the average employee?
4. Is the company serious about inculcating its philosophy and values at all levels of the organization?

Some companies produce their own form of business creed. Management Support Systems collaborated with the King-Bay Chaplaincy to produce "A Business Creed for Corporate Excellence" as an example of a concise form of statement. (A copy of the Business Creed is reproduced in Appendix 4.)

A more comprehensive list of corporate values and standards follows as a suggested guideline for analyzing existing statements of philosophy or as a framework for developing one for your company. There are five key areas of value analysis to consider: (1) Human worth, (2) Justice, (3) Stewardship, (4) Community, (5) Leadership style.

1. *Human Worth*. In all matters of policy, decision, and action does management
— value people above things?
— recognize people as the key resource of the company?
— treat employees with love, dignity, and respect?
— foster the personal growth and development of the employees to their full potential?
— foster creativity and innovation?
— provide meaningful work?
— value long-term employment and job security?
— give priority to the health and safety of the employees?

2. *Justice*. In all matters of policy, decision, and action does management
— exercise fairness and justice?

— manifest corporate responsibility and ethical conduct?
— produce high-quality goods and services to meet authentic needs?
— give priority to customer service?
— pay fair wages and equal pay for equal work?
— reward diligence and excellence?
— provide equal opportunity for advancement?
— insist on no-discrimination?
— share information openly and honestly?

3 *Stewardship*. In all matters of policy, decision, and action does management
— exercise responsible stewardship?
— make good use of the human resources of talent and skill available?
— make responsible use of the limited resources of the earth?
— treat the environment with care and respect?
— balance high technology with human values?
— enable the employees to share in the company's success and have a sense of shared ownership?
— respect the culture and customs of other nations?

4 *Community*. In all matters of policy, decision, and action does management
— foster co-operative community in the organization?
— build trust and team spirit?
— foster open and effective communication?
— build a climate of acceptance and belonging?
— foster interdependence and the freedom to share personal feelings?
— minimize social distinction?
— foster company loyalty?
— foster labour-management trust and co-operation?
— provide for recreation, fun, fellowship, and *shalom*?

5 *Leadership Style*. In all matters of policy, decision, and action does management
— manifest appropriate and effective leadership styles?
— value and encourage a servant-leadership style?
— enable subordinates to take responsibiilty and develop their potential?

— encourage participation in decision making and problem solving?
— clarify the decision-making process at all levels?
— foster the corporate community spirit?
— show equal concern for the needs of the employees and the tasks to be accomplished?
— develop a shared sense of responsibility for the success of the operation?
— set an example of high standards?

Operating Norms

The end result of the application of the company purpose, identity, and philosophy is the *Operating Norms*, the standard operating procedures, and the traditions which express "how we live and work together in this organization."

A healthy organization has a healthy spirit in which its purpose, identity, philosophy, and norms are integrated and expressed with consistency and integrity. On the other hand, an organization in which there is discontinuity and lack of connection between these elements is spiritually unhealthy and will be characterized by confusion, lack of commitment, apathy, conflict, and decline. For an organization to remain healthy and vital it must constantly keep alive its sense of identity, renew its purpose and goals, and be open to new ways of operating.

Organizational Health

Once they understand the management model and how it works, Christian lay people, no matter at what level they work in the organization can have some influence on the spiritual vitality of the organization. Obviously, the higher up they are in the company, the more influence they can have. Significantly my research indicated that a high percentage of senior managers are active church people. If these people felt supported by the church and their fellow Christians in the organization, they could be encouraged to express their spiritual values more openly in the processes of corporate decision making. Even at a comparatively junior level, one person I know was able to transform an uncaring and dehumanizing department into a community with a friendly and co-operative spirit. He consistently treated everyone with love, dignity, and respect.

At the King-Bay Chaplaincy, Management Support Systems has developed a management diagnostic instrument called a Value-Analysis Profile (VAP). It is a means of gathering data on the values operating in key functional areas of corporate life so that management strategy and policy can be based on the desired values, and motivational and moral problems which adversely influence performance can be clearly identified. If, for example, there is a divergence between the values of managers and staff, causing discord and hindering co-operative productivity, the Value-Analysis Profile would reveal the problem and its cause. If the executive management of the organization decides that it is desirable to clarify its corporate culture, and improve the *esprit de corps* as a means of achieving corporate excellence, the VAP-feedback-process would provide the data for intelligent planning.

The following Management–Strategy Analysis is a way of quickly identifying the areas of organizational life which are most in need of value analysis. Instructions follow to explain the process.

Management-Strategy Analysis

(Rank the following elements in order of importance to the effective operation of the organization)

(Rate each element on the scale in terms of its present strength and effectiveness)

___(1) **Corporate Purpose or Mission** — All levels of management able to articulate "The business we are in, and our service to society."

12345678910
low   high

___(2) **Corporate Sense of Identity** — Management having a clear sense of "Who we are as a company" and its uniqueness.

12345678910
low   high

___(3) **Corporate Philosophy & Culture** — A widespread awareness of the values and beliefs which motivate and guide the organization.

low 1 2 3 4 5 6 7 8 9 10 high

___(4) **Corporate Sense of Community** — Having a commitment to a spirit of co-operative community throughout the organization.

low 1 2 3 4 5 6 7 8 9 10 high

___(5) **Management Leadership Style** — The management leadership style is appropriate and fosters co-operation and productivity.

low 1 2 3 4 5 6 7 8 9 10 high

___(6) **Organizational Structure** — The structure of the organization reflects the philosophy, values, and leadership style of management.

low 1 2 3 4 5 6 7 8 9 10 high

___(7) **Human Resourcing** — Policies based on the value of persons and the development of their potential.

low 1 2 3 4 5 6 7 8 9 10 high

___(8) **Labour-Management Relations** — Priority given to the development of mutual trust and co-operation between labour and management.

low 1 2 3 4 5 6 7 8 9 10 high

___(9) **Technological Development and Utilization** — A healthy balance is achieved between human values and technological efficiency.

low 1 2 3 4 5 6 7 8 9 10 high

___(10) **The Operational System** — The operating norms, policies, and procedures are in harmony with the philosophy and values of management.

low 1 2 3 4 5 6 7 8 9 10 high

Instructions for the Management Strategy Analysis:

Part 1

For the first part of the exercise, use the left-hand blanks only and ignore the scales on the right-hand side. Read carefully the ten elements of the management system. As you do this, visualize

what is happening in your company in each area and how it affects your organization. Rank each element in order from 1 to 10 depending on its relative importance in the effective operation of the organization.
Note: we are not asking which elements are the most efficient or productive, but which contribute the most to the effectiveness of the whole company. The most important is ranked 1, and the least important is ranked 10. Give each element a ranking number.

Part 2
In the second part of this exercise use the right-hand scales on the form and rate each element as a separate entity. Rate it in terms of its present strength and effectiveness. On the first item, if you feel that all levels of management in your company are proud and excited about the corporate purpose or mission and are able to articulate it in a way which will inspire company loyalty, then you would rate it high and give it an 8 or 9. For each element be as objective as you can.

Part 3
Reflect on the high and low ratings on the right-hand side and relate them to the rankings on the left-hand side. Do your high ratings correspond with the elements you have marked as most important to the effective operation of your company? What are the implications of the low ratings for your organization? Can you identify any areas of potential ill health in your organization? How might this effect the strategic planning of your company?

If, for example, you found that managers ranked number three (Corporate Philosophy and Culture) as very important to the effective operation of the company, but the rating of their present strength and effectiveness in this area was only a 2, you have probably identified a source of much confusion, friction, and poor communication in the organization.

I suspect that most managers would be at a loss to know what to do about that situation, because in most cases they would have to guess (a) at how the employees perceive the operative values in the organization and (b) what the preferred or ideal values of the employees might be. Without objective data of this kind, management is likely to waste a lot of time and money with hit-and-miss attempts to improve the situation.

The Value-Analysis Profile
The Value-Analysis Profile (VAP) is a management diagnostic instrument. It provides the means to gather data on the ideal values of employees and the values that are generally operative in their organization. The most significant information provided by the VAP is the size of the gap between the actual operative values as perceived by the employees, and the ideal values by which they would prefer to work. Where the gap is large there will probably be conflict or resistance to management. This data will identify opportunities for improvement in organizational performance and provide a basis of understanding on which to develop management improvements.

Each VAP focuses on one of the ten key elements of the management model and consists of a series of opposite value perspectives on the issues, concerns, and functions related to that particular element. For every aspect of management, there is usually a polarity of value-based attitudes or positions. There are values and attitudes based on the traditional Adam Smith ideology, and there is a different set based on the new emerging values, most of which, from a Christian perspective, are closer to the values of the kingdom of God. The following is a sample of a typical VAP question (each profile contains about twelve value contrasts of this type). (A complete set of the Value-Analysis Profiles is included in Appendix 5.)

Competitive individualism is the driving force within our organization	Presently 0 1 2 ③ 4 5 6 7 8 9 ──────────────────────── 0 1 2 3 4 5 6 7 ⑧ 9 Ideally	Trust is the basis of co-operative community in our organization

In the scoring process the number circled on the top line indicates the way the scorer feels things are, presently, in his or her company. The number circled on the bottom line represents what this person feels would be the achievable ideal in this company. (The statement on the left side expresses the traditional values, and the one on the right side expresses the emerging values.)

In the example, the person rating the value perspective feels that competitive individualism is largely the way things function in the organization, so he rated the top line at 3. He would like people to relate on the basis of trust and co-operation, so he marked the bottom line at 8. In this case the gap is four units on the scale. We regard three or more units as significant and five or more as critical. If the average gap for the department was four units, it would clearly indicate that a change in management philosophy was required, because there is a direct relationship between the size of the gap and the degree of employee motivation and productivity.

Instruments such as the Value-Analysis Profile may be used as a management consulting tool in a corporate system to provide feedback to senior management as a basis for strategic planning or policy. It could also be used by an individual or small group of Christians who want to get a clearer understanding of the values and trends in their organization, so that they can be more intentionally Christian in their own choices and decisions. We have discovered, in using the VAP questionnaires, that they raise the consciousness of values and help people to clarify their own value system.

Changing Values

Our values are changing. The following is a comparative list of some of the traditional values which have shaped our business system and some of the emerging values which I believe are more in harmony with the values of the kingdom of God.

Traditional Values	*Emerging Values*
Mechanical Images	Personal Images
More Money	Job Satisfaction
Career Advancement	Meaningful Work
Recognition	Good Health
Community Status	Domestic Happiness
Achievement and Success	Job and Financial Security
Competition	Co-operation

Autocratic Style	Participation
Individualism	Team Work
External Controls	Internal Controls
Independence	Interdependence
Efficiency	Good Relationships
Profit	Service
Big is Better	Human Scale
Centralized Power	Decentralized Power
Consumer Society	Conserver Society
Man's World	Equality of Sexes

This list is not intended to imply that one set is all good and the other all bad. Many of the traditional values are still good and necessary; however, the emphasis is shifting. When times are tough, the emerging values tend to be put on hold, and companies operating on a *lean-and-mean* basis tend to prefer traditional values. This may be appropriate as a short-term experience; however, I believe that in the long term the new values will provide the creativity and motivation essential for corporate excellence.

Questions for Personal Reflection or Group Discussion

1 Does the decription of value-based management and the ten-point model provide a helpful frame of reference for the development of your own ministry of applying kingdom values in the workplace?

2 Use the values and standards listed on pages 78-80 for each of the five key areas of value analysis as a checklist to evaluate your company's performance from a value perspective. Identify the areas where you feel that you might be able to exercise some influence and reinforce the kingdom values.

3 As a group, use the Management-Strategy Analysis form on pages 81-82 to reflect upon the life of your organization, and to determine where you might try to introduce some changes. Also compare the corporate philosophy. Compare with statements in Appendices 2, 3, and 4.

4 In what ways do you think that the data produced by the Value-Analysis Profile method would help you to exercise a

Christian ministry in your organization? Use a selection from the ten VAP's in Appendix 5 to analyze your work situation.
5 Use the contrasting lists of traditional and emerging values on pages 85-86 to reflect upon the changes taking place in your organization. In your planning, which values do you tend to emphasize?

6
Community in the Workplace

Genuine community is the highest achievement of mankind, it demands more of us than any other endeavour, and it is supremely worth the struggle. Elizabeth O'Connor

If then our common life in Christ yields anything to stir the heart, any loving consolation, any sharing of the Spirit, any warmth of affection or compassion, fill up my cup of happiness by thinking and feeling alike, with the same love for one another, the same turn of mind, and a common care for unity . . . Look to each other's interest and not merely your own. Philippians 2:1-4

Christianity and Community

Human beings were created for community by the God whose own experience is a unity of love and sharing with the Son in the fellowship of the Holy Spirit. Community is therefore an essential ingredient in our quest for genuine humanity. "You can't be human alone."

Whatever is at the centre of a community determines its character. Christian community has a special quality of life because Christ is at its centre. It is the fulfilment of Jesus' promise, "Where two or three have met together in my name, I am there among them."[1] The unity of community was high on Jesus' agenda. He prayed to his heavenly Father for his followers, that they may "all be one: as thou, Father, art in me, and I in thee, so also may they be in us, that the world may believe that thou didst send me."[2] The building of community is at the heart of the life of the Christian church and the ability to build it is one of the greatest gifts the church has to offer a divided world.

The fact that the church has manifested so much disunity is probably one of the main reasons why the world is so slow to believe in Jesus as Lord. It is also an indication of the power of evil to be able to sow discord even among the people of God.

In spite of our failures, the power of the church has always been its loving and caring community. In fact, whenever the church has been really effective, it has manifested the kind of community that has made it the visible body of Christ. This is always the work of the Holy Spirit, the "go-between God" who is able to take an ordinary group of very fallible men and women and weld them into a loving and caring community. One of Saint Paul's favourite greetings sums it up: "The grace of the Lord Jesus Christ, and the love of God, and the fellowship (or community) in the Holy Spirit, be with you all."[3]

Community is essential to the life of families, cities, and nations; its presence is critical to the survival of any organization, church, or business. Yet, because it is an intangible thing, we tend to take it for granted. Simply getting people together, either in a church or the workplace, does not produce community. It is a question of the quality of the relationships and the depth of the communication. If people live or work together over a considerable period of time, a sense of community will tend to develop. However, in our fast-moving world, there is seldom time for more than superficial relationships, and we don't very often really know, trust, or care about one another. This means that we have to be intentional about building community. First we must believe that it is important enough to give it priority in planning and managing our organizational life; then we must know and understand the dynamics of interpersonal relationships and actively facilitate the process.

When I was director of a church conference centre, I was able to combine a background in human relations and group dynamics with the biblical theology of Christian community. On many exciting weekend events my colleague, the Reverend Douglas Blackwell, and I witnessed the transformation of congregational groups into trusting and caring communities. The program we developed was published as a manual, *Experiencing Christian Community, A Program Manual for Christian Community Development in the Local Congregation*.[4] The knowledge and experience gained from this program was transferred to the much more difficult environment of the business community when the King-Bay Chaplaincy was developed.

When one sits in a little office in the midst of the great office towers in the business district of a large city, one feels isolated and alienated. In this highly materialistic culture the economic bottom line is the driving force of the system. As my secretary Ruth Cartwright and I thought about the nature of our ministry, we faced the question, Should we be a counselling service, doing the ambulance work of picking up the casualties caused by the system? Or should we attempt to penetrate the system and try to influence it from a Christian perspective? We chose the latter route; although, of course, counselling is part of our ministry. Using our knowledge of community building we have managed to build a network of Christian business people of all denominations who identify themselves as friends of the Chaplaincy. Many of them are learning how to be more intentionally Christian in their daily work, with a sense of ministry which can turn a desk into an altar.

Community is a basic human need and essential to the well-being of any organization. However, in a free and pluralistic society it is not realistic to expect to build a specifically Christian community within a particular company or organization. But the basic principles of community building can be applied in any situation. In other words we can do theology without speaking theology or using religious terminology. God does not need credit lines when we perform acts of love.

This principle has been powerfully demonstrated in Operation Bootstrap, our program for unemployed business people. Within a few days of intentional community building, we see men and women for whom competitive individualism had been a way of life transformed into a mutually caring and co-operative community. They are committed to helping each other deal with the trauma of unemployment and to finding or creating a job. Because the program is open to people of all backgrounds and faiths, we do not use religious language. But when we affirm the dignity, worth, and ability of individuals who have experienced months of rejection and discouragement, it is an expression of Christian love and caring.

Building Community

The guiding philosophy behind community is that people are stronger together than they are separately. The origins of the word reflect this spirit; it comes from the Latin *communis*, which is composed of *com*, meaning "together," and *munis*, meaning, "ready to be of service together," and that implies not only being in the same boat, but pulling in unison on the oars.

Community develops within an organization when there is an environment of trust, in which mutually supportive and caring relationships can develop, and co-operative and creative action is fostered.

The story is told of a management consultant who was doing some work in South America when he happened to visit a boys' orphanage run by a Roman Catholic priest. After a few days of observing the behaviour of the boys, he was most impressed with the happy sense of community among them. So he asked the priest what was the secret of success in building that kind of community. He replied that there are five simple things that are essential for community. First of all, people must have *something in common* that brings them together, a common need, or purpose, or belief. As orphans the boys had a basic need in common. Secondly, they must have a sense of *security*. They knew that they had a safe and permanent home, where they belonged and were accepted. Thirdly, there must be a sense of *equity* or fairness. The boys all knew that there were no favourites, they were all treated with equal love and respect. Fourthly, their *individuality* was respected, their differences were accepted and valued. Fifthly, we encourage *participation* by the boys in the decisions that affect them. These five principles can form the basis upon which programs can be designed to build corporate community.

Levels of Community

There are three levels of community, each with a different level of intensity of relationships, and each requiring different forms of nurture and development.

1 The small group
The basic building block of community is the small group of six to twelve people. In these numbers people can really get to know each other at a significant level, through trust and open communication. The quality control circles used so successfully in Japan are based on the dynamic of the small group. Responsibility and authority is given to help the group to solve its own problems and control the quality of its output.

Using the small group as the basic building block, it is possible to achieve a high level of community even in a large organization, by linking the groups together in an integrated network. If an individual has a strong sense of participation and belonging in any part of an organization, he or she can identify with and be loyal to the whole company.

2 The departmental unit
This would include groups of up to fifty people. The unit is still small enough to have its own identity within the larger whole. The right kind of leadership can help to build an *esprit de corps* within the department, including friendly competition with other departments.

3 The whole organization
This is largely the responsibility of the chief executive officer who articulates the company purpose and image and inspires pride in the organization. There are many types of company activities such as social programs, employee assistance programs, sponsorship of sports teams, which can produce a general sense of community. However, the small group remains the key to significant community, and the remainder of this chapter is devoted to understanding the small-group process, as a means of exercising an important lay ministry in the workplace.

The Community-Building Process

Many sophisticated approaches to organizational development are based on very simple principles. For example, Robert Blake developed the *managerial grid* and applied it to every aspect of management. It is based on the recognition that when a group has a job to do, the leader of the group must take into account two basic components: the concern for task, and the concern for people. The job must be done and the needs of the people in the work group must be met if they are to function productively.

The concern for people includes maintaining group functions such as interpersonal relationships, listening and communication skills, and agreed-upon group standards, so that the group members know what is expected of them. It also includes the recognition of the individual needs of members in the group who have concerns about how they are perceived by the others, how much power and influence they may have, whether or not they are accepted by the group, and who the real leaders are. If these needs are not met, a great deal of valuable time and energy can be wasted because of unhealthy group dynamics such as distrust, competitiveness and jealousy, lack of confrontation, and unresolved conflicts. These produce high levels of stress and lower productivity.

The effective leader or manager gives equal attention to the other component, the task. Here again a number of particular group skills are required: problem solving, decision making, and goal setting.

The effective manager shares leadership functions and coordinates the group by taking initiative, making suggestions, gathering information, and summarizing and testing for consensus.

If both of these components are not dealt with in an intentional manner, building an effective working community is likely to be a long and painful process. I have found that the best way to build trust and facilitate group development is to take time to help members set standards and reach a consensus on how they want to function as a group. Depending on the circumstances, communication exercises which encourage a measure of personal sharing of life journeys quickly develop mutual understanding and caring and the willingness to take risks together.

The following diagram indicates the community-building process, which moves from the personal- and group-maintenance functions to the task functions. A group will not survive if it does not have some sense of accomplishment or achievement. Being an effective group member or leader provides plenty of opportunity for the exercise of an enabling and caring ministry.

The Community-Building Process

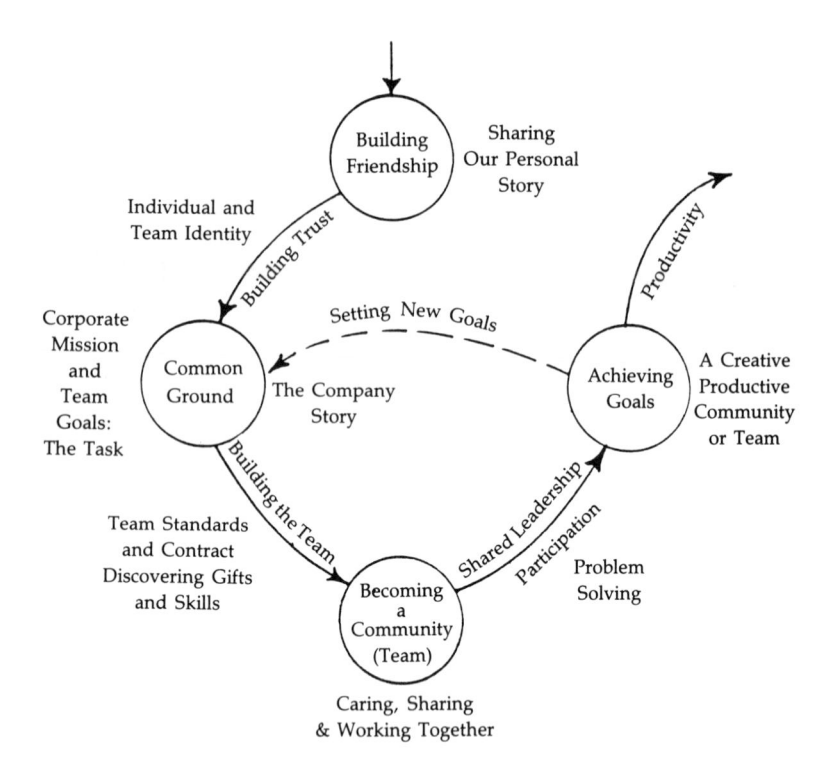

```
                    Building          Sharing
                    Friendship        Our Personal
                                      Story
    Individual and          ᴛ
    Team Identity    ɢ  Trust
                  Building
    Corporate                Setting New Goals
    Mission                                              A Creative
    and      Common   The Company      Achieving        Productive
    Team     Ground     Story            Goals          Community
    Goals:                                              or Team
    The Task      Buil                   Shared Leadership
                      ding                                Productivity
    Team Standards        the                     Participation
    and Contract            Team                        Problem
    Discovering Gifts          Becoming                 Solving
    and Skills                    a
                              Community
                                (Team)
                    Caring, Sharing
                    & Working Together
```

Community-Building Checklist and Planning Guide

The following community-building checklist may be used in two ways. It can be a means of evaluating the level of community in your present workplace, and then become a basis for planning ways to strengthen the sense of community. The list of characteristics is designed to evaluate the quality of community in a work group, but it may also be applied to the organization as a whole. Rate each characteristic according to the following scale:

1 — Poor, very little success in this area.
2 — Fair, considerable improvement is needed.
3 — Good, there is room for some improvement.
4 — Excellent, the group is functioning very well in this area.

1 Common ground
__ *Common Purpose, Interest and Commitment*
The work group is committed to a common purpose or task which it feels is important and worthwhile.
__ *A Strong Group Identity*
The group takes pride in having a special identity and reputation for excellence.
__ *Common Assumptions and Shared Values*
The group has clearly understood standards of operation and behaviour and a sense of shared values and priorities which are in harmony with the values of the organization.

2 Security
__ *High Level of Trust*
Group members have learned to trust each other, in an atmosphere of openness and honesty. They have a sense of mutual responsibility and loyalty to the group.
__ *Mutual Caring*
There is a family feeling of acceptance, belonging, and mutual caring in the group. Members feel free to share personal needs and find emotional support.
__ *Continuity and Long-Term Relationships*
It takes time to develop genuine community. Group members need job security, a sense of continuity, and a reasonably long-term commitment to the group.
__ *Their Own Turf*
Most groups like to have their own "turf," a workplace in which they feel some ownership.
__ *Incorporation of New Members*
Care is taken to incorporate new members by sharing the culture of the group, its standards, and values.

3 Equity
__ *Standard of Fairness*
The group maintains a standard of fairness and justice. All members know that they will be treated fairly and equitably. Their opinions are listened to and respected.
__ *Shared Responsibility*
The members feel mutually responsible for the quality of the group life and its productivity.
__ *Open Communication*
Open and direct two-way communication is maintained at all levels of the organization. The group knows what is going on and how the company is doing, and it keeps others informed of its own situation.
__ *Recognition and Reward*
Recognition and rewards for performance are given to the group, rather than to individuals, so that there is pride in the group accomplishment. *We* did it!
__ *Minimum Social Distinction*
Social distinctions between levels of authority and responsibility are minimized to avoid the kind of barriers which inhibit team spirit. Friendly informality and direct communication are characteristic of relationships at all levels.

4 Individuality
__ *Respect for Individual Difference*
The group recognizes and respects individual differences in personality type, gifts, and skills. These are affirmed and valued as complementary contributions to the synergy of the group.
__ *Opportunity for Personal Growth*
The company recognizes the individual's needs for personal growth, provision is made for ongoing training and development, and members of the group are encouraged to change roles and learn new skills.
__ *Role Clarity*
Although flexibility and rotation are encouraged, the roles, responsibilities, and accountability of each member are always made clear.

5 Participation

___ *Mutual Decision Making and Consensus*
Members of the work group are consulted and share in decisions which affect their work. Decisions pertaining to the group as a whole are made by consensus.

___ *Group Problem Solving*
Members are taught and encouraged to use group problem-solving and planning skills and methods which utilize the knowledge and variety of gifts among the members.

___ *Creative Risk Taking*
An entrepreneurial spirit is encouraged, and permission is given to take risks and to fail, without penalty. Training is given in the use of imagination and creative thinking. New ideas are taken seriously and rewarded in direct relationship to the benefit to the company.

___ *Balanced Concern for People and Task*
An effective community maintains a balanced concern to get the job done well and efficiently, with the concern to meet the needs and aspirations of the group members. The ethic is "The work is as important to the worker as the worker is to the work."

Having rated your group or company on the above characteristics of community, total the rating numbers.

Point Range	Indications
20 – 40 points—	Indicates a generally poor level of community and low productivity. An outside consultant is recommended.
40 – 60 points—	Indicates considerable room for improvement, and a consultant could be helpful. Check to see if your work group is particularly weak in any one of the five key elements of community, and plan for improvements in that area.
60 – 80 points—	Indicates that your group is above average and should be performing well.

The secret of the success of Operation Bootstrap has been the direct application of the principles of community building. Unemployed people in small co-operative community groups, using these principles and the basic skills of job search and creation, can solve their own unemployment problems. The co-operative team approach really works! The process of moving from the stress of uncertainty and powerlessness to empowered planning removes the main causes of debilitating stress and releases the energy they need to get the job or to start a new business.

Labour—Management Co-operation

Labour and management have traditionally operated on the assumption that their relationship is always and inevitably adversarial. Certain vested interests maintain this adversarial relationship to justify their type of confrontational leadership. This approach is obsolete, ineffective, and unchristian. Obviously labour-management antagonism and conflict destroy the possibility of co-operative community. I believe that it is the responsibility of Christians and other concerned people to work for a change in the system by encouraging union-management co-operation.

In an article in the *Harvard Business Review*, Donald Scobel, director of the Creative Worklife Centre, provided some guidelines to ensure that experiments in union-management co-operation would withstand the test of time. In the article, "Business and Labor — from Adversaries to Allies," he says, "America's economic problems reflect . . . a breakdown in the systems traditionally used to manage the workplace. A lasting solution . . . . means that, among other things, unions and companies must steer away from their adversary stance toward a more cooperative relationship."[5] Scobel points out that during the recent recession many changes were made in the direction of co-operation, but he is concerned about effecting permanent change. He found that some of the most encouraging signs of progress occured when high-level plant managers and union officials went together on retreats, usually away from the plant site and often in a nearby community. During a two- to four-day session, the participants discussed the personal implications of case studies drawn from other co-operative efforts.

It is important to emphasize that the objective is not to eliminate unions, but to change the relationship from adversary to ally in the joint enterprise of a successful business. Trust has to be earned, and it usually involves taking risks and being vulnerable. This is the only path to reconciliation which really works. Spiritual principles and values which put people and co-operation first are the ones that work best, whether or not they are consciously motivated by religious beliefs.

In an article in the *Toronto Star* (April 1985) David Crane reported on the results of a study of the Swedish system which applies spiritual values in business and industrial operations.

> Sweden's success in achieving harmonious labour relations also holds important lessons for Canada. Our record on labour relations shows 598.1 working days lost per 1000 workers on average each year in 1981-83 compared to just 19.5 days lost in Sweden. Strikes are costly and also generate ill feelings in the workplace that are damaging to companies.
>
> In Sweden labour unions, which represent about 85 per cent of the workforce compared to 39 per cent in Canada, have directors on the boards of companies, access to company information and must be consulted on all changes affecting the members. Swedish industry also makes widespread use of quality circles and various programs that permit workers to organize their work activities and job content.
>
> The result is that Swedish workers have considerable participation in the management of companies, the second highest in the industrial world according to the European Management Forum, while Canadian workers have little participation, in fact one of the lowest in the industrial world.
>
> Canadian industry, with some exceptions, is characterized by mistrust between management and unions. Many Canadian businesses are hostile to unions and unwilling to consult with employees, share information such as opening the company's books, or allow employees to experiment in ways of organizing their jobs.
>
> As a result of their high level of participation, Swedish workers have a much higher level of motivation than Canadian workers, identifying strongly with their employer's objectives.[6]

Most of the Swedish success is due to the application of the kind of spiritual values which are in harmony with a Christian perspective; their application does not depend upon political socialism. Co-operation can work just as well in our political and economic system. If the powers-that-be, many of whom are active church people, would relate their Christian perspective and values to the way they direct and manage their business, they could transform not only the business community but also our society.

Donald Scobel says that "transforming a relationship from adversary to cooperative requires a company to demonstrate its trust in employees by reevaluating old rules and regulations. Otherwise, labor will charge that management is paying lip service to the cooperative effort."[7] He quotes a union representative as saying, "Improving people's work lives is the guts of unionism. For years, we went after wages, hours, and so on. Now we're moving toward trust and dignity. To me, saying that cooperation can hurt our ability to represent people is a cop-out. All I know is that when we all try to get along, we get fewer employee complaints and we are more in tune with our members." On the management side, Howard Carlson, director of quality-of-work-life research for General Motors, said that all of GM's efforts at union-management co-operation had a sense of excitement about them. This reflects Scobel's view that, "once cooperation establishes roots, spirits rise, information flows, some restrictive policies change, and people who have never met after working 30 years at the same place become colleagues on committees."[8] This should encourage Christian managers and unionists to work towards co-operation and community building as an exciting form of ministry.

Questions for Personal Reflection or Group Discussion

1 How do you respond to the statement that "the building of community is at the heart of the life of the Christian church, and the ability to build it is one of the greatest gifts the church has to offer a divided world"?
2 Do you feel that it is worth trying to build co-operative community in the workplace, even though it is not feasable to make it a specifically Christian community?

3 As a group, use the Community-Building Checklist and Planning Guide on pages 94-97 to assess your own performance and identify where changes may be necessary. The problem-solving process from Chapter 8 may be used at this point to develop a plan of action.

7
Business Ethics and Social Responsibility

Determining the balance between commitment to profitability and commitment to society is a managerial decision and one which has yet to be fully worked out in a satisfactory manner in the business community. . . . Robert Boulanger and Donald Wayland

Ethics and Morals

It is important to make a distinction between ethics and morals. Morals involve observing *mores,* customs and good manners. Written and unwritten norms — this is not acceptable; this is acceptable — are expressions of good morals, which may differ from one culture to another and from one corporation to another. Being a good citizen means,"When in Rome, do as the Romans," and keep within the law. Ethics, on the other hand, involve universal principles and values. Oppression and injustice may not violate any particular moral framework. But from a Judeo-Christian perspective, the right to freedom and justice is a binding ethical value which applies to every form of human life. The apartheid laws of South Africa are an obvious case in this point. This is where the values of the kingdom of God take precedence in the hierarchy of values.

Business people often face agonizingly difficult decisions. For example, some might think it a good thing for a powerful Western company operating in a third-world country to teach its workers to read and write. Others might ask, Does an individual company have the right to interfere in a country's social policies; is this not capitalist imperialism? The answer is not easy. Should a Canadian company in South Africa pay blacks and whites equal wages, when this is not the policy of the local government ? A white South African might consider discrimination morally acceptable but from a Christian point of view it is ethically unacceptable. A company employing Christian ethics would want to work out a policy based on long-term achievement of justice in its African plant.

Corporate Ethics

In his book *Management of Values—The Ethical Difference in Corporate Policy and Performance*, Charles McCoy of the Pacific School of Religion and Centre for Ethics and Social Policy, in Berkeley California, points out that implementation of corporate values is now recognized as a primary responsibility of executive management.

Dr. McCoy notes the increased concern with ethics in recent years in schools of business administration and management and among thoughtful executives in leading corporations. He gives the following reasons for this increasing interest in ethics.

> First, concern with moral issues in the business community clearly derives in part from well-publicized stories of bribery, fraud, and questionable practices by corporations and corporate executives. . . . Thus, the interest in ethics comes from a perceived need among executives to maintain a good public image of business.
>
> Second, concern with ethics among business leaders derives in part from the heightened standards of performance applied to most societal institutions, corporations as well as others. . . .
>
> Third, the rising interest in ethics derives not only from external pressures. It comes in part from the genuine concern of many executives for the well-being of society . . . .
>
> And fourth, corporate executives want to be good at their jobs. Increasingly, it is becoming clear that excellence in managing and performance demands attention to corporate culture and values and that policy making requires ethical insight and moral courage as well as technical know-how and organizational skills.[1]

Every company has two types of ethical responsibility: internal and external. Because I believe that most Christians in the business community have an opportunity to exercise an intentional Christian ministry, the primary focus of this book is upon the ethical responsibility of an organization for its own internal operation and management. However, an important potential for ministry at the executive level would be ignored if we did not consider the relationship of Christian values to the external or corporate social responsibility of companies.

Macro-Ethics

Corporate social responsibility has received a great deal of public attention recently. There is growing public concern demanding answers to ethical questions: questions relating to justice for workers and all those affected by company policy and operations, questions regarding pollution, environmental concerns, and the wise use of non-renewable natural resources. These are macro-ethical concerns on the global scale.

This is a relatively new development. Previously business operations were regarded as ethically neutral. Their function was to produce and sell, and thereby create job opportunities for employment. The business of business was business. Many business executives in the past found it safest to restrict themselves to the company's functional responsibility, basing their decisions solely on business principles, such as production and marketing prospects. The moral and ethical concern was primarily micro-ethics, the honest and fair behaviour of individuals in the organization.

Today it is no longer enough to be a Christian in your personal business dealings. Your company might be damaging the environment, harming human life, taking advantage of powerless people, and exploiting them. There is complicity by association, and those in responsible positions cannot simply play the game by the old rules.

Ludvig Jonsson, a Swedish Lutheran minister and chief executive of the Institute for Work Ethics in Stockholm, in an article on corporate codes of ethics wrote, "Whether we like it or not, these [ethical] questions are being raised today. They are being raised not only by journalists using a slanted approach, but by the employees, by the general public, by those who buy the firm's products or who hold one or two of its shares. The big question is this: Has capitalism any ideology ?"[2]

Today a considerable shift from the traditional stance of laissez-faire capitalism demonstrates a growing willingness of business to share in the responsibility of helping to solve society's problems. My survey indicated that managers generally agreed that corporations should be socially responsible bodies. In fact, twenty-seven per cent strongly agreed, and sixty per cent partly agreed that "business should assume public responsibilities even at the cost of reduced profits." This is a significant level of consensus which should encourage top management to give leadership in this direction.

In an address to the Toronto Board of Trade, Mr. E.M. DeWindt, chairman and chief executive officer of the Eaton Corporation (U.S.), said that "business people have to go beyond the narrow concerns of their business and take an active role in shaping public policy. The days of the cloistered chief executive are gone. . . he can no more delegate the responsibility for involvement in the shaping of public policy than he can delegate responsibility for the profitable operation of his enterprise."[3]

Very few people are equipped to think and function adequately in the field of macro-ethics. When referees of various kinds blow the whistle and cry foul, there is a natural tendency to indignation on the part of those who are honest and fair-minded people on the personal micro level. Macro-ethics shifts the focus onto the world picture, and property rights, power, and control take on a new significance in a finite global village.

It is only natural that companies are reluctant to make unilateral changes which involve economic sacrifice. They are willing to change if everyone else does the same. This is why it is usually necessary for government to legislate such changes.

The Trade-Off Process

Most of the mainline Christian denominations have recently been actively involved in a dialogue with major corporations about social justice. When the church and Christian individuals in the business community try to influence the ethical decisions of companies, it is essential that they understand the complexity of the managerial process. It is too easy for church groups to propose social goals without suggesting how they should be accomplished, because in some cases only undemocratic means or force could bring them about.

Harold A. Gram, professor in the Department of Management at Concordia University in Montreal, in an article, "The Churches and Corporate Life," states that "socially responsible behaviour and any kind of corporate behaviour are affected by the ethics and values of the managers, but also by the nature of the corporate processes, the nature of the trade-off process, and the selection of the means to accomplish results and goals. . . . The corporate manager functions within an environment which has its own values and standards."[4]

Decision making in business is often characterized by trade-offs between good and better, good and worse, or better and best. The business person has to take into account the often conflicting rights of the many groups which have a legitimate stake in the operation: the owners and stockholders, the board of directors, the public and customers, the employees and the union. Managers are unwilling to assume personal responsibility for decisions on social goals and assess their economic costs against the business, unless the decision is objectifiable and defensible before these other stakeholders. Decisions often have to balance conflicting goals, preferences, and demands.

In the difficult trade-off process managers are often caught between the conflicting interests of environmentalists, the unemployed, shareholders, and social activists. How does a company decide which in the long term is the best policy — to invest and provide jobs or to boycott and put pressure on the government to reform? "Those who make demands for desirable actions but ignore the dimensions of the trade-off process and provide no ethical and moral guidelines for making choices are irresponsible."[5]

Stewardship, a Basis for Macro-Ethics

I believe that the biblical doctrine of stewardship provides the most comprehensive framework for the development of a macro-ethic for nations and multinational corporations. It is based on the belief that "the Earth is the Lord's and all that is in it" and people were created to be responsible stewards or managers of the earth's resources, according to the will of God.

The function of the company is to employ capital so that it grows. However, the *means* by which the profitable growth is achieved is an ethical concern. We do not have the right to economic growth at any price whatsoever. It is not ethically defensible for a firm's assets to be allowed to grow at the price of semi-slave labour in South Africa, or at the price of health hazards to the employees in production, or at the price of unnecessary plant closures for the sake of greater profit elsewhere.

Also the company's stewardship is not limited to the invested capital. The company is also entrusted with extensive human resources: the capacity of the employees, their health and security, their opportunity to function as full citizens. Work is not only a form of production, it is a community of people. Economic stewardship must be balanced with social stewardship. When we get down to basic principles, the things that really matter are love and stewardship. We are called to relate to people with love, justice, and mercy, and to relate to everything else — time, energy, ability, and material things — as stewards or responsible managers for the good of all humankind. Saint Paul in his letter to the church in Ephesus wrote, "Live life, then, with a due sense of responsibility, not as men who do not know the meaning and purpose of life, but as those who do."[6] And Saint Peter said, "Above all, keep your love for one another at full strength" and "whatever gift each of you may have received, use it in service to one another, like good stewards."[7] As members of decision-making groups at various levels in the company, Christian people have a responsibility to help the group members reflect upon the assumptions and values behind their decisions, and uphold Christian values.

Ethical Decision Making

The rule of thumb then in ethical decision making is first to ask, Is it the loving thing to do? and secondly Is it the responsible thing to do? Of course, the two are often interrelated; so that the stewardship of a material source is also the loving thing, as it affects the lives of people.

The most difficult decisions are usually not between the good and the bad, but between two relative goods in the hierarchy of values. The values of love and stewardship are usually mutually supportive, but sometimes they conflict, when some course of action would honour the rights of one group but infringe on the rights of another. In this case the decision makers would have to decide which action would result in the greatest good.

The following diagram illustrates the source of many ethical dilemmas.

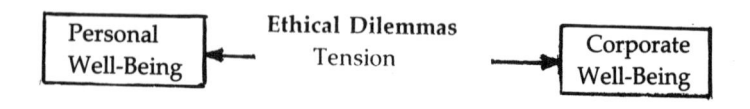

```
┌─────────────┐    Ethical Dilemmas    ┌─────────────┐
│  Personal   │ ←─     Tension      ─→ │  Corporate  │
│ Well-Being  │                        │ Well-Being  │
└─────────────┘                        └─────────────┘
```

Personal Values

Human Rights
Caring Relationships
Justice
Freedom
Jobs
Fair Wages
Meaningful Work
Dignity and Respect
Co-operative Community
Personal Objectives
Safety and Security
Employee Health
Open Communication
Participation
Personal Growth
Servant Leadership
Human Touch
No Discrimination

Corporate Values

Property Rights
Goods and Services
Ethical Conduct
Use of Resources
Economic Viability
Fair Profit
Productivity
Quality and Worth
Competitive Market
Corporate Purpose
Efficiency
Environmental Care
Public Accountability
Market Share
Economic Growth
Leadership in Society
High Technology
Honest Business

What does a manager do when faced with the dilemma of laying off loyal employees or going out of business in an economic recession? To keep the employees on would be a caring act, but to allow the firm to go out of business would be bad stewardship. The obvious solution is to apply the principle of "tough love." In the most compassionate and just way lay off the minimum number of employees; then work hard to recover the business and rehire those laid off.

"First-order" thinking is the obvious course most often taken by management. However, in the above situation, if management had been trained in "second-order" thinking, they might have reframed the problem, not as a company problem to be solved by management on behalf of the shareholders, but as a personal problem for all those who work for the company. The problem would have been shared openly with all the employees, and brainstorming sessions held to create alternatives to the obvious layoff solution. When their jobs are at stake people can be incredibly creative in reducing production costs, finding new uses for the product, and in developing new markets or new products. On this basis, I believe that many plant closures could have been avoided and jobs saved or created.

The spirit of an organization has a lot to do with the way corporate decisions are made. The philosophy of the company will determine the attitude to people and profits. How decisions are made reflects the outlook and training of those making the decisions. For example, executives who have been trained to monitor the finances of an organization and ensure that it stays within its budget are not inclined to risk breaking out of this framework with creative and innovative ways of operating.

Robert Greenleaf feels that the failure of business leaders to use foresight and take creative action before a crisis arises is tantamount to ethical failure, because they lack courage to act when there is the freedom to change course. They are often forced to make reactionary decisions because the options previously open are now closed. Greenleaf says that "by this standard a lot of guilty people are walking around with an air of innocence that they would not have if society were able always to pin the label 'unethical' on the failure to foresee and the consequent failure to act constructively when there was freedom to act."[8]

However, executive decisions can only be as good as the quality and type of information upon which they are based. Many corporate information systems tend to supply data to the decision makers on a rather narrow basis, such as production and finance related to profit. Data which reflects the spirit of the organization and is sensitive to ethical considerations and the changing values and trends in society is essential for the development of foresight. However, this kind of data will only become a part of the information process when it is seen as a priority by senior executives.

Corporate Codes of Ethics

In an article entitled "Social Goals for Canadian Business," L.J. Brooks Jr. of the Faculty of Management Studies, University of Toronto, points out that, "due to the heightened social awareness of executives and continuing pressure from society, Canadian corporations must increasingly act not only within the law but also ethically in the eyes of those now recognized as having an interest or stake in the company." To avoid the displeasure of their stakeholders, executives are attempting to manage their companies' social performance more effectively."[9] In response to a survey by Brooks, many of Canada's 125 largest corporations indicated that they were developing statements of corporate social objectives to assist in the management of their social performance. Such companies as Alcan, TransCanada Pipelines and the Toronto Dominion Bank have published codes of ethics. The Toronto Dominion Bank requires all employees twice a year to sign a document declaring that they have read, understood, and complied with the code. Standards include honesty, integrity, loyalty, confidentiality, limits on gifts, payments, conflicts of interest. I believe that such codes of ethics represent a significant step forward, and no doubt will in time have a considerable effect on corporate performance and image. However, there is still a long way to go in this process. In response to the question in my survey of management values, Do you feel that there should be some form of public reporting of corporate social responsibility?, twenty-seven per cent said, "Yes," forty-two per cent said, "No," and thirty-one per cent said, "Possibly."

There is always the risk that such a code of conduct will be so general and watered down in its content that few will regard it as binding. There is also the danger that once it has been published, the code will be placed in a drawer and possibly serve as a text for speeches on special occasions. Ethics are more than rules and regulations; ethics reflect an attitude which results in action. Business ethics are effective only if company values are discussed and its actions are reappraised.

The Centre for Ethics and Social Policy in Berkeley California has identified what it considers to be three basic and interrelated elements of a comprehensive corporate ethic.

1 Corporate self-interest
This is not only basic but legitimate for any individual or corporation and survival and success depend upon it. There is of course a difference between enlightened self-interest (the stewardship of corporate resources) and selfishness and greed. The difference is usually determined by the spirit of the organization and its ethics. The organization must have a clear understanding of its own interests and purpose. But this must be broadened and related to other ethical perspectives.

2 Multiple responsibility
The relationships between a corporation and the many groups affected by it are essentially ethical in nature. A corporation which actively considers the needs and claims of those whom it affects, and offers some form of accountability, is pursuing the ethics of multiple responsibility. This often requires the balancing of conflicting demands and requires considerable ethical awareness and sensitivity.

3 Social vision
This third element concerns ways in which the future of the larger society is envisioned. A broad social vision includes both national and global perspectives and ensures that the macro-ethical implications are taken into account. It involves having a vision of a desirable future in the light of changing values and human needs.

Unless we acknowledge the authority of a higher power, to whom all people are accountable, sooner or later institutions, whether they be nations, states, or multinational corporations, will usurp the power of God in human affairs. For those who share Christian convictions, the biblical values and images of the kingdom of God provide the ideal criteria for our decision making, whether we are involved in internal or external corporate concerns.

The elements of ethical decision making for corporate responsibility are combined in the following model which provides a rational framework for a complex process.

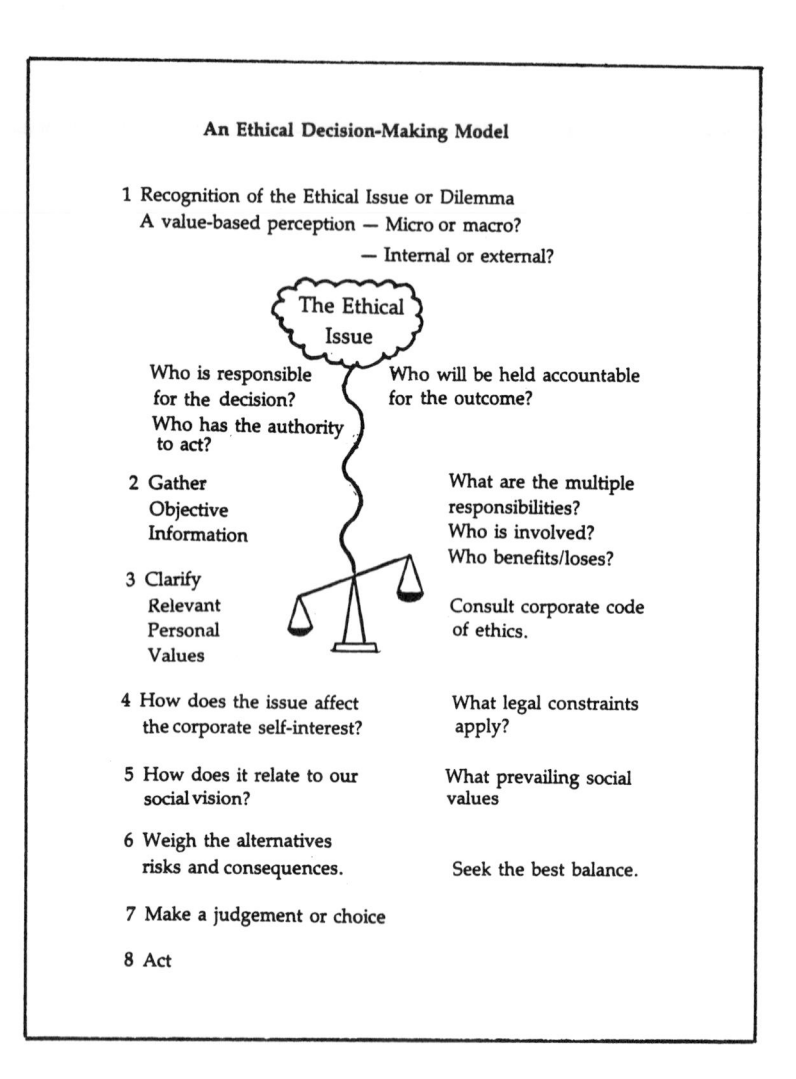

An Ethical Decision-Making Model

1 Recognition of the Ethical Issue or Dilemma
A value-based perception — Micro or macro?
— Internal or external?

The Ethical Issue

Who is responsible for the decision?   Who will be held accountable for the outcome?
Who has the authority to act?

2 Gather Objective Information

What are the multiple responsibilities?
Who is involved?
Who benefits/loses?

3 Clarify Relevant Personal Values

Consult corporate code of ethics.

4 How does the issue affect the corporate self-interest?

What legal constraints apply?

5 How does it relate to our social vision?

What prevailing social values

6 Weigh the alternatives risks and consequences.

Seek the best balance.

7 Make a judgement or choice

8 Act

The Objective
The objective of ethical decision making is to arrive at a decision which is:

— *Logical* — does it make sense in the light of the data?
— *Legal* — does it meet the standards of society?
— *Fair* — does it take into account the rights and needs of all concerned?
— *Ethical* — is it right and just in light of our highest values?
— *Humane* — is it the loving thing to do?

The Social Audit

A further step beyond the code of ethics is the social audit which allows companies to measure social performance in quantifiable terms. Corporate executives can monitor not only the production and economic performance of the company but also social and ethical performance. The audit may be conducted internally or by an outside group. Social responsibility accounting usually includes the following four levels:

1 Inventory — a descriptive summary of activities performed.
2 Program summaries — a summary of objectives and activities plus an assessment of success.
3 Cost statements — programs or activities with cost attached.
4 Cost-benefit analysis — costs to the company compared with benefits to society.

The relatively few Canadian companies that have used the social audit have found that management became more sensitive to social issues that affected the corporation, and the process was beneficial to them. My survey indicated that thirty-two per cent felt that the social audit was a good idea and should be widely adopted, fourty-two per cent felt that the idea should be widely tested, and twenty-six per cent felt that it would be a waste of time.

The First National Bank of Minneapolis publishes an annual *Social-Environmental Report* which documents and illustrates not only the social value of its banking operation but its environmental, philanthropic, and employee investments. This includes an indication of the time and effort of the employees in community involvement.

For those who may want to pursue this approach, I have included in Appendices 13 and 14, a set of criteria for evaluating public-affairs issues (produced by Human Resources Network of Philadelphia), and a comprehensive basis for a social audit (produced by the Centre for Public Resources, Inc. in New York).

The benefits of including this kind of value-related information in corporate management and planning are:

1. It would enable management to maintain a healthy spirit within the organization. The use of instruments such as the Value-Analysis Profiles described in Chapter 5 would provide an internal value audit which would undoubtedly have some bearing on the financial audit statements.
2. A periodic social audit of the company's performance in the field of social responsibility would tend to broaden the vision of the decision makers and increase the number of policy alternatives available and the flexibility of action.
3. A knowledge of value trends would enable the decision makers to be more pro-active regarding future needs for products and services.
4. The personal satisfaction of the decision makers would be increased and it would enable them to provide more confident moral and ethical leadership as an organization, with a consequent improvement in the public attitude toward business.

Questions for Individual Reflection or Group Discussion

1. To what extent do you feel that attitudes towards corporate social responsibility by both the public and corporate leaders have changed in the past fifteen years? What kinds of change have you noticed and why do you think they are happening?
2. Do you agree that social ethics is a complex process, and that the church needs to be more sensitive to the necessary trade-offs which business must take? What kind of ethical guidelines could the church provide for both the desired ends and the means by which ethical decisions might be achieved?

3 As you reflect upon the lists of values related to personal and corporate values on page 108 can you think of situations in your own experience where there has been conflict between the two? How did you handle the situation?
4 Does your company have a code of ethics? If yes, review it from a Christian value perspective. If not, you might consider raising the issue with senior management and provide information on the matter.
5 Does your company conduct a social audit? If not, you might begin by making your own analysis of the company's social performance, using Appendix 14 as a guide. This might provide a basis for discussion with senior management on the possibility of a more formal approach.

8
Creative Problem Solving

For anything new to emerge there must be a dream, an imaginative view of what might be. For something great to happen there must be a dream. The venturesome persons with faith in that dream will persevere to bring it to reality. Robert Greenleaf

A Christian View of Problem Solving

The ability to solve problems is one of the most important human characteristics. It has enabled us to produce the agricultural, industrial, scientific, and communication ages, to cure disease, and reach for the stars. It is the way we master and shape our environment, our society, and ourselves. It is not a mysterious process, available only to a few; we all use it every day: the child doing her homework, the mother planning tomorrow's lunch, the businessman financing a new project, or the scientist overcoming the force of gravity to put a man on the moon are all solving problems. The process in each case is basically the same; the only difference is the degree of complexity and the sophistication of the technique. By solving problems we learn and develop as rational human beings.

If I want to be able to build a boat or make a dress, fix a leaking tap or invest in the stock exchange, I begin with a gap between what I already know, and what I need to know. The gap is my problem, and I will go through a process of information gathering and idea finding until I solve my problem and achieve my objective. If I am able to think creatively, I may devise a new and better way of doing what has to be done. This is creative problem solving. The process itself is neutral; it can be used to achieve good or bad objectives. To the robber a bank robbery is a problem to be solved. To the doctor a disease is a problem to be solved. The process can be used to design an X-ray machine or build an atomic bomb.

You may wonder what this has to do with Christianity. Our faith perspective or value system is an integral part of our problem solving. The way we perceive the problem in the first place is determined by our values. Two people with different values may face the same situation; one will perceive a problem requiring change, while the other will think everything is satisfactory. Some people feel comfortable paying women less than men for the same work; others do not. This is a matter of value perspective. But values lead to behaviour, and so problem solving involves making decisions and choices between alternative courses of action. By applying Christian values to organizational problem solving, we have the power to initiate a preference for caring and responsible activity in the workplace. The principles of love and justice are sometimes very different from the goals of the short-term bottom line.

Of all the ways of translating faith into action I have learned over the years, Christian value-based problem solving is the most widely applicable and practical. *It is a primary tool for lay ministry.* It is a matter of learning how to *think* as a Christian. We are to cultivate the mind of Christ. In other words, in our problem solving we are to try to think as Jesus might have done. But it also requires a conscious intention to act as a Christian in our decision making. The process works like this:

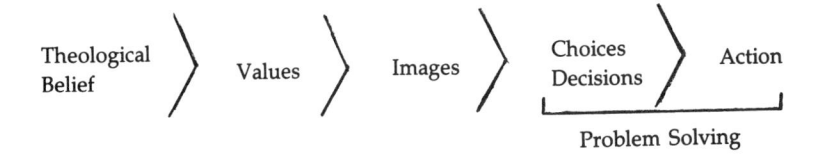

Theological Belief ⟩ Values ⟩ Images ⟩ Choices Decisions ⟩ Action

Problem Solving

Problem solving and opportunity planning are two sides of a coin and involve the same process. Creative people see every problem as an opportunity to improve things or to create something new. The problem of communication produced the telephone, and the problem of diabetes produced insulin. We can see problems and plan to solve them, or we can see opportunities and plan to meet them. The steps required are the same.

Creative Thinking

Creative thinking is a rare commodity in the business world, and its rarity makes it a highly prized talent. Computers are obedient, fast, accurate, and they have terrific memories, but they do not have the creative imagination or sensitivity to truth and beauty that is uniquely human. That is why companies compete fiercely for "idea people" and are happy to pay them premium salaries. Yet despite the demand for such people, few in business and industry have any clear understanding of what creative thinking is. Still less do they realize that it is a skill which any reasonably intelligent person can learn.

The study of creativity is comparatively new. Before 1950 only a few people had seriously investigated the creative process, and most believed that it was the prerogative of the gifted few. However, it is now recognized that with understanding and practice, people can increase their creativity and problem-solving ability to a considerable extent. Scientists tell us that the human brain has more than twelve billion cells capable of storing and processing information. But we usually use only a small percentage of this creative potential and there is plenty of room for development.

One of the pioneers in investigating the creative process is Sidney J. Parnes, professor of creative studies at Buffalo State University. He says that, "creativity is a function of knowledge, imagination, and evaluation. The greater our knowledge, the more ideas, patterns, or combinations we can achieve. But merely having the knowledge does not guarantee the formation of new patterns; the bits and pieces must be shaken up and interrelated in new ways. Then the embryonic ideas must be evaluated and developed into useable ideas."[1] The creative process is rather like a kaleidoscope. Our knowledge is like the little bits of coloured glass which, when the drum is rotated, form an infinite number of beautiful patterns. Each new pattern is like an idea.

Much has been learned about the creative thinking process and how the left and right hemispheres of the brain function in different but complementary ways. Yet the actual "spark" of creativity remains a mystery. We can all improve and develop our creative ability, but there will always be some people who stand out as having special gifts of insight and creativity.

Where does the spark come from? I believe that all creativity comes from God the creator. Being made in his image, human beings reflect a godlike creative capacity. We can imagine something that does not exist and then create it as a physical reality. This is how the writer of the epistle to the Hebrews described creation: "By faith we perceive that the universe was fashioned by the word of God, so that the visible came forth from the invisible."[2] The Creator Spirit is the agent of divine creativity in the universe, and through prayer and meditation it is possible to tune in on that creative power. This power is available to and operates in anyone who is open to it, regardless of particular beliefs.

But our beliefs influence our perceptions. Much of the art of problem solving is based on the way we perceive the problem. Faith enables the creative person to break out of traditional molds and risk imagining the new. There is a link between spirituality and creativity, and we need to learn how to draw on the source of creative power. Fortunately creativity is not dependent upon intelligence, age, or education. Our creativity is dependent upon

— our awareness and powers of observation,
— our curiosity and ability to see things in new ways,
— our ability to abstract and to break down problems into component parts,
— our ability to synthesize and put existing things together in new and unexpected ways,
— our flexibility and willingness to accept change, to abandon old assumptions and ways of thinking.

Most people try to solve their problems by working harder at the old way of doing things. This is called "first-order" thinking, and sometimes it is the best thing to do. Creative problem solving opens the unexpected possibility of working or thinking differently. This is called "second-order" thinking. When we first identify a problem we tend to see it within a particular frame of reference, and this determines how we go about trying to solve it. Second-order thinking involves the ability to leave the usual frame of reference to gain a new perspective on the problem.

There is a popular perception game in which nine dots are arranged in a square and the participants are challenged to see if they can connect all nine dots with four consecutive straight strokes of a pencil, without raising the pencil from the page.

• • •

• • •

• • •

Most people automatically try to stay within the frame of the box, although that was not a given condition. Within the frame a solution is impossible; but as soon as the lines are extended beyond the frame, the problem is easily solved. This is second-order thinking.

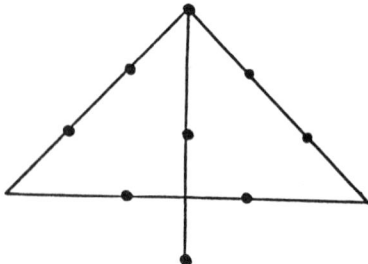

Left-and Right-Brain Thinking

Recent studies on the way the human brain functions have opened up a whole new understanding of our thought process.

The brain consists of two distinct hemispheres, joined by a communication cortex. The left hemisphere controls the right side of the body, and the right hemisphere controls the left side of the body. Generally speaking, the left brain functions rationally and logically, and uses words to describe what it sees. It names things, counts, analyzes, and figures things out on a linear step by step basis. The right side of the brain is primarily visual and nonrational. It thinks in pictures. It is intuitive and sees things whole. It is the source of artistic ability, and forms images and integrates ideas.

For a variety of reasons, including the fact that the majority of people are born right handed (controlled by left hemisphere), our society and the education system have developed the use of the left brain to a greater extent than the right. And we have tended to reward left-brain more than right-brain behaviour. We tend to rank left-brain scientific method and engineering logic more highly than the right-brain aesthetic contribution; yet many of our intuitive leaps forward in grasping truth have come out of the right-brain function. There are also indications that direct mystical experience of God, the "religious experience," is apprehended by the right brain. The left brain wants a rational proof of the existence of God, whereas the right brain just wants to commune with divinity.

The computer is a logical product of the left brain, and is increasingly taking over the rational functions in our society — data processing and calculation by formula. Much of what I learned as an engineer can now be done faster and more accurately by a computer. It is interesting to speculate about the long-term effects of the computer on human consciousness. As it relieves us of much left-brain thinking, we may develop an increased use of our creative and spiritual capacities. Perhaps science and religion will be integrated, and the next stage of human development will be spiritual.

The ideal is to develop and use both sides of the brain equally. We need both if we are going to turn dreams into reality. *Creativity* is the generation of new and novel ideas; *innovation* is the systematic process which transforms ideas into products and services. Creativity tends to be an individual process, whereas innovation is almost always a collaborative enterprise requiring the co-operation of numerous individuals. The composer writes the score but the conductor leads the orchestra to play it. The inventor creates the concept, but it requires an innovative entrepreneur to get it produced and on the market.

The Creative Process
Creative thinking is a two-stage sequence. First there is a divergent thought process which opens up the mind and

generates ideas. This is followed by a convergent process which evaluates the ideas and selects the best ones for solving the problem.

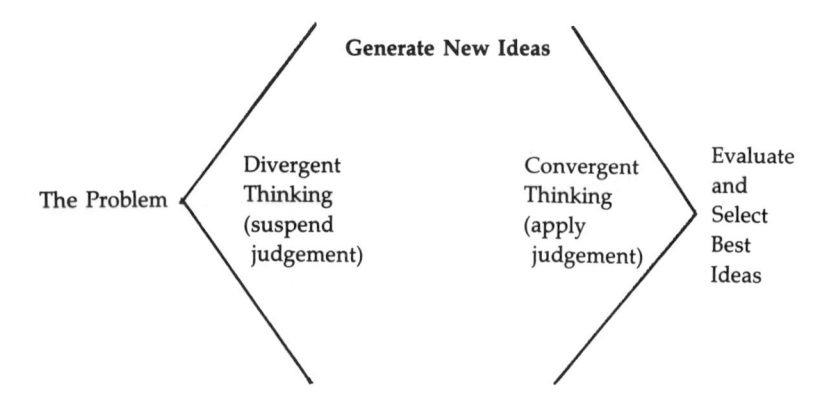

```
                    Generate New Ideas

                 Divergent          Convergent      Evaluate
                 Thinking           Thinking        and
The Problem      (suspend           (apply          Select
                 judgement)         judgement)      Best
                                                    Ideas
```

The creative process is often called brainstorming; it uses both left- and right-brain ways of thinking. It also uses a process which Edward deBono, one of the world's foremost teachers of creative thinking, calls "lateral thinking." The brain stores information on the basis of association. It is as if all associated ideas are put in a mental file folder, and when one idea is pulled out of the file, related ideas tend to come with it. This is vertical thinking. Lateral thinking occurs when in random, non-linear fashion, the mind jumps laterally to another mental file folder and a whole new train of thought develops.

Brainstorming is usually done with a group who are interested in solving a particular problem, Once the problem is clearly defined, its cause understood, and a clear objective is established, the group is encouraged to call out ideas as they occur. The ground rule is that all judgement or critical comment is suspended, to avoid inhibiting the flow of ideas. For the first while, vertical thinking usually operates and there is a flow of associated ideas; then the flow stops and there is a temptation to stop the process at that point. However, if the group persists, lateral thinking will probably begin and a host of new ideas, usually the best ones, will be generated. Finally, when ideas have run out, the critical faculty is used to evaluate the long list that has been recorded. The idea that seems most likely to achieve the objective and solve the problem is then selected.

In sorting out the creative possibilities produced by divergent or lateral thinking, a Christian value perspective can beneficially influence the choice of action, service, or product. One of the graduates of our Bootstrap program provided an illustration of this process. Hans Burger is a talented man with the unusual capacity of being able to use both the creative imagination of his right brain and practical organization of his left brain to transform his ideas into practical reality. He is well educated, with degrees in engineering, architecture, and law. But he was unemployed. He had worked for a large construction company but when high interest rates caused the company to close, he was without a job. Like most people, he tried to get back into the business he knew, but after months of fruitless search he grew discouraged and lost his self-confidence, and finally turned to Operation Bootstrap for help. In the course of our seminar, we do a simple risk-taking exercise which helps people to reflect on their own willingness to take a risk and try a new approach to life and the job search. In the middle of the exercise Hans had an "ah ha!" experience. Why depend upon others for a job? Why not start his own business! Discouragement changed to enthusiastic optimism, and he has since started several successful new businesses.

But there are some other things we need to know about Hans, because they relate to the type of businesses he developed. Hans has a strong humanitarian value system. He has been very active in the Boy Scout Movement at all levels, and he is concerned about helping handicapped people. One day, following the Bootstrap seminar, he was walking along a street in the city when he happened to notice a barber raising the level of his chair with a foot pump. Nothing unusual about that, but it sparked a serendipity experience which resulted in an exciting new business. Hans continued his journey on a subway train and, while thinking of nothing in particular, his right brain made a lateral connection. He suddenly thought, "Why don't I design a table which can be pumped up and down so that handicapped people who have difficulty getting food up to their mouth can rest their elbows on the elevated table and so feed themselves? He went home and designed a motor-driven table which has since been sold in several countries. Hans opened a plant employing about a hundred people. Among his employees he hired several young people recently released from jail, people who normally have great difficulty getting a job.

Hans is full of ideas, and as soon as he gets one he transforms it into a business. But notice the part played by his value system. His concern for the handicapped brought the problem and the solution together, and his concern for young people created jobs for some of them.

We serve a wonderful God who, like Jesus, does not give us pat answers to our problems or our prayers, but expects us to think for ourselves and to use the creativity he has given us to identify and solve problems as co-creators with him.

If we combine this creative thinking with logical problem-solving we have a valuable tool to deal effectively with any kind of problem we may face. Once we learn the method and discipline ourselves to use it, it will serve us for the rest of our lives and provide a practical way of applying our Christian faith.

A Creative Problem-Solving Process

The first concept to grasp in problem solving is to see the problem as the *gap* between the *ideal* and the *actual* situation.

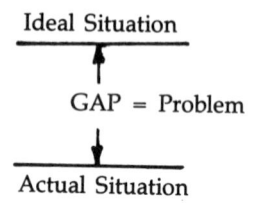

```
         Ideal Situation
        ─────────────────
                ↑
          GAP = Problem
                ↓
        ─────────────────
         Actual Situation
```

In our discussion of first- and second-order thinking, we discovered that problems do not have to be negative situations, but can become opportunities for improvement. We often miss an opportunity because we accept the present situation as normal or inevitable. With imagination, it is often possible to visualize a better or ideal situation. Then we recognize the need or the gap and begin to think of what we could do to close the gap and change the situation. That is creative problem solving.

Study the following flow chart to get an overview of how the step-by-step process works.

Creative Problem-Solving Process

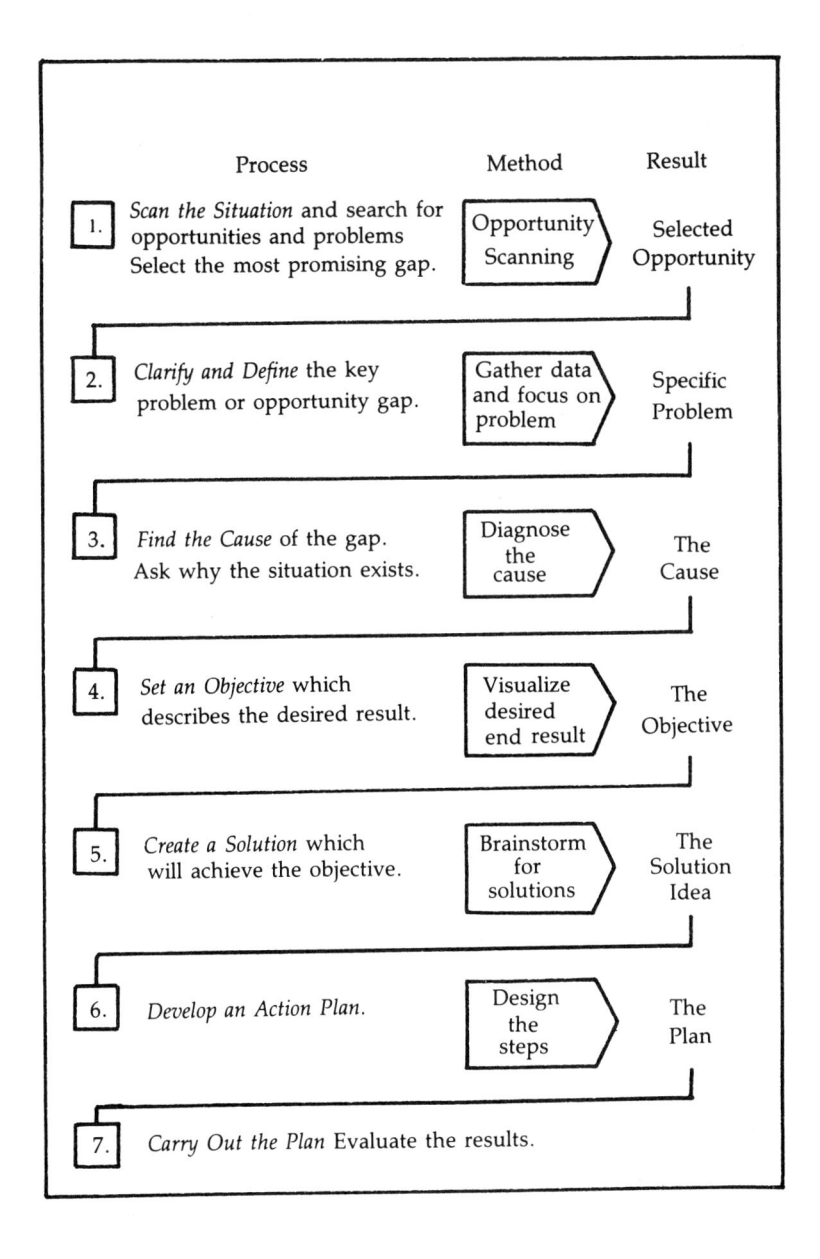

	Process	Method	Result
1.	*Scan the Situation* and search for opportunities and problems. Select the most promising gap.	Opportunity Scanning	Selected Opportunity
2.	*Clarify and Define* the key problem or opportunity gap.	Gather data and focus on problem	Specific Problem
3.	*Find the Cause* of the gap. Ask why the situation exists.	Diagnose the cause	The Cause
4.	*Set an Objective* which describes the desired result.	Visualize desired end result	The Objective
5.	*Create a Solution* which will achieve the objective.	Brainstorm for solutions	The Solution Idea
6.	*Develop an Action Plan.*	Design the steps	The Plan
7.	*Carry Out the Plan* Evaluate the results.		

The key to the process is not to wait for problem/opportunities to confront us but to search for them. This is the first step in the process.

1 Problem opportunity search
Scan the situation and search for problems (gaps) and opportunities. Select the problem or situation which represents the greatest need or holds the greatest promise for creating something new. This involves divergent thinking to explore all possibilities and then convergent thinking to select the most promising opportunity as illustrated below.

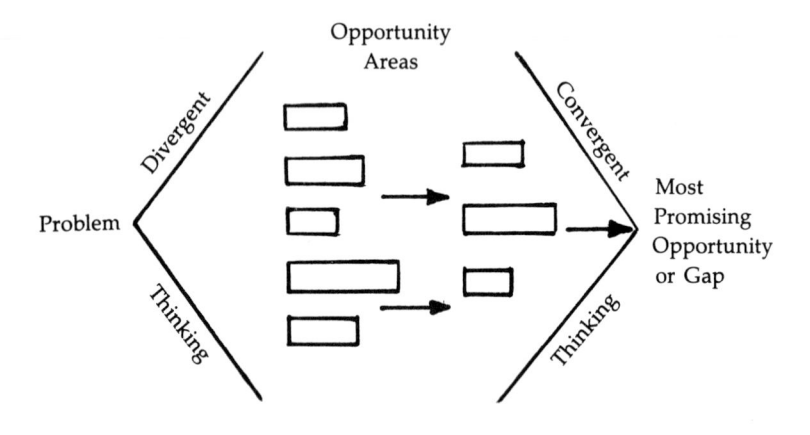

The following scan questions are designed to prompt your imagination.

— what has changed in this situation?
— what needs are not being met?
— what is not working well?
— what disturbs or excites me?
— what is the gap in this area?

This first step is like walking through an art gallery, looking at the pictures. Pick a few that really grab your attention and interest, and then narrow them down to the one you want to buy.

By way of illustrating the total process, I will use an actual medical case. It would apply equally well to a business or personal problem. Ten years ago attention was focused on the fact that some premature babies were born with a disease called Respiratory Distress Syndrome (RDS). There was no known cure and about thirty-six per cent of the babies survived only for a few days after birth. Step one was the decision to do intensive research on this particular problem.

2 Clarify and define the key problem
Focus on the situation; ask what precisely is the problem or need. Gather information, get the facts. What data is available? Who else might know something about it?

A common mistake at this point is not to distinguish between single and multiple problems. It is seldom possible to find one solution to a group of problems. Break multiple problems into single or simpler problems that you can do something about. For example, the high cost of housing is a multiple problem. The way to break it down is to keep asking Why? The answers will point to the sub-problems. Housing is a problem because of

— the high cost of land
— the high cost of materials
— the high cost of labour
— the high cost of mortgages.

Each sub-problem would have to be dealt with separately. And you would begin with the one with the best potential for cost reduction.

In the medical example, research showed that the newborn babies had increased difficulty breathing and finally their lungs collapsed. There was evidence that the hyaline membranes in the lungs were not performing properly; oxygen was not getting through to the blood stream. The problem had been specified.

3 Find the cause
You cannot solve a problem until you have accurately diagnosed its cause. If the problem is a new situation, the following questions may help you to find clues to the cause.

— when did it first occur, and what was happening at that time?
— who or what was involved?
— what changed in the situation and why?
— what are the symptoms, and are there any analogous situations?

Millions of dollars have been wasted trying to solve business and industrial problems simply because this step was neglected or given inadequate attention and someone guessed at the cause. Band-aids do not solve problems.

In the medical case, further research revealed the cause of the problem. The baby's system was not producing a substance called "surfactant," which lubricates the membranes and enables the oxygen to pass through for effective breathing. The precise problem was then, What can be done about the lack of surfactant?

4 Set an objective
An objective is a description of the desired end result. At this stage it is important to consider how you are going to achieve it, because this short circuits the process. Visualize your objective and then describe it according to the following criteria. The objective must be

— specific
— measurable
— achievable
— challenging
— completed by a certain date.

Values play an important part in setting the objective. Does the end result, as you have described it, reflect your Christian values? To be enjoyable and worth doing, the job would probably involve direct or indirect service to people.

In the medical example, an objective might have been to reduce the infant mortality rate due to Respiratory Distress Syndrome by seventy-five per cent within two years. This is specific, measurable, achievable, challenging, and completed by a certain date.

5 Find the solution

This is the most creative part of the process; you brainstorm all the possible solutions to the problem, and then select the one(s) that will most effectively achieve your objective. It must deal with the cause and solve the problem.

Sometimes the brainstorm produces one great idea which will meet the objective; but it is more likely to produce a number of ideas which, when incorporated into a plan, will achieve the objective. Again, the selection of the ideas will reflect your values and priorities. One possible solution might put economics first; another might put people first. Your role might be to convince the group that long-term human benefit is more important than short-term gain.

The following solution-finding questions will encourage ideas.

— what could we do better?
— what could we do differently?
— what could we make more cheaply?
— what could be simplified?
— what could be made smaller or larger?
— what could be adapted for other uses?
— what could be combined with other things?
— what missing element could we provide?

When you are brainstorming, it is important to observe the principle of visibility. As the ideas are called out by the group, they must be written on newsprint or a blackboard. Ideas are fleeting and will soon be forgotten if not recorded. As the eye travels back over the list of ideas, certain words will stand out and trigger new thoughts. Remember the brainstorming rules.

1 Generate the maximum number of ideas as fast as possible.
2 Let your ideas be as wide ranging or "far out" as you wish.
3 Suspend judgement, no questions asked.
4 Hitchhike on other ideas.
5 Keep going when you first think you have run out of ideas, lateral thinking will then open new streams of thought.

When you run out of ideas, switch to convergent thinking and select the best idea or combination of ideas.

In the medical case, many different approaches were tried to deal with the cause of the problem. It was decided to concentrate on finding a means of enabling the body to produce its own supply of surfactant necessary to keep the lungs functioning normally. The research proved successful and the drug Celestone was found to effect the cure. The babies were enabled to survive the first few critical days until their system functioned normally. The mortality rate for babies with the disease is now about six per cent, a reduction of about eighty-three per cent in the past ten years.

Miracles are still happening. Jesus said, "In truth, in very truth I tell you, he who has faith in me will do what I am doing; and he will do greater things still because I am going to the Father. . . . If you ask anything in my name I will do it."[3]

Modern medicine is curing diseases which didn't even exist in Jesus' time. We are fortunate he has given us the creative ability and the continuing inspiration of the Holy Spirit to guide us into all truth, both scientific and spiritual.

6 Develop an action plan

Once you have your basic solution idea, it is relatively easy to put it into a logical step-by-step plan with a time schedule. As you answer the following questions, the plan will take shape.

— *how* will we implement the solution idea(s)?
— *what* steps will be involved, and how long will each step take?
— *who* will be involved?
— *when* will we do it?
— *where* will it be done?
— *what* resources will we need?

Write out your plan and critique it to find the weak spots, so that you can make adjustments to ensure success.

7 Carry out the plan and evaluate the results

Evaluate the results in the light of your objective. Did you achieve it? Did you deal with the cause of the problem? Has the problem gap been closed?

I should point out that problem solving is seldom as neat and tidy as the above would indicate. Quite often you will get part way through the process and discover an even more pressing problem which must be solved, so you go back to step one and work through the process again. However, when a group succeeds in solving a problem or meeting an exciting opportunity, there is a great feeling of accomplishment, and for some, a creative ministry will have been performed.

For practice, why not gather a group of people who want to learn how to apply their faith on the job, and use the above process on some of the case studies in Appendices 6-11.

Questions for Personal Reflection or Group Discussion

1. How would you explain the statement that "Christian value-based problem solving is a primary tool for lay ministry"? What is the connection between perception, decision making, and values? (Luke 12:13–31: see how Jesus perceives an inheritance problem and proposes a value-based solution.)
2. Do you believe that all creativity comes from God? What are the implications of this belief for those who have a close relationship with God in prayer and meditation?
3. What are the implications, for Christians, of the new understanding of the different functions of the left and right hemispheres of the brain? For example, does an overly rational (left-brain) approach to liturgy and worship inhibit a more right-brain response to God? Would more opportunity for spontaneous music and dance, together with the use of modern visual techniques, be more in tune with the way people think and experience today?
4. As manufacturing processes are shifted to the Third World, the future of our society and its standard of living will increasingly be dependent on our creativity, innovation, and ability to adapt to change. Most world religions have a static "rear-view mirror" concept of God that is locked into past revelation and makes it difficult to accept change. How does the Christian understanding of the ongoing and dynamic leading and guiding of God the Holy Spirit equip Christians to ac-

cept change and move into the future with creativity and confidence?
5   Study the Creative Problem-Solving Process on page 125 and use it to develop solutions to the case-study problems in Appendices 6-11. Then use it regularly on your work-related problems. You might also find it helpful in developing programs in your local church.
6   Use the instrument Scanning Your Work Environment in Appendix 12 to discover some of the ways in which you can minister to the spirit of your organization. Then use the problem-solving process to close some of the gaps you discover.

9
The Ministry of the Laity

The strategy of Christ was to win the loyalty of the few who would honestly respond the new way of living. They would be pioneers of the new order, the spearhead of advance against the mass ignorance, selfishness, evil "play acting" and apathy of the majority of the human race. The goal which was set before them, for which they were to work and pray — and if need be suffer and die — was the building of a new Kingdom of inner supreme loyalty. The Kingdom of God.
J.B. Phillips

Ministry in the Church

The New Testament makes it quite clear that Jesus empowered and commissioned the church to be the continuation of his body on earth, and it is the whole membership of the body that is to continue the ministry and mission of Christ in the world. There is thus only one Christian ministry, the ministry of Jesus Christ. He calls every baptized member of his church, ordained and lay, to share in his ministry in the world.

The use of the term *laity* can be misleading; for some people it implies non-professional or second class. In fact the term is derived from the Greek word *laos* which means "the people," and consequently both clergy and non-ordained church members belong to the laos or people of God. However, the term laity is a convenient way of distinguishing between the two orders, and as used in this book, it simply refers to the ninety-nine per cent of church members who are not ordained but who, by virtue of their baptism, have a front-line ministry of their own. The ordained clergy have a key role to play in the order and sacramental life of the church, but the ministry is a shared function of the whole body.

The evolution of an ordained ministry is apparent in the New Testament. In the earliest writings such as Paul's letters to the Corinthians, there is no indication of any specific person or group being in charge of the young churches. There is the primary ministry of the apostles — the twelve, and others including Paul — some called apostles, some co-workers, some prophets —who were travelling missionaries who established new congregations, and had ministries to more than one local church.

In due course, it became evident that an ordered and authoritative leadership was required; the apostles were dying, and long-term organization was necessary. "In the book of Acts and the later epistles, we see the beginnings of an ordained ministry. . . . Bishops were the chief of these and their role was similar to that of the apostles; they presided over the community. As the church spread to include a larger area with several churches, the bishops appointed elders (priests). Assisting the bishop, administering the church's funds and serving the needs of the poor, were the deacons. All these soon became full-time paid occupations. . . . A process of clericalization had begun which gradually gathered up all the ministries of the church into itself. . . . The people were gradually reduced to a basically passive state. The ordained tended to become full-time givers and the laity full-time receivers."[1]

The Reformation challenged this clericalization, but only the more radical Protestant denominations actually gave the ministry back to the people. "The professionals continued to dominate and the people were happy to have it so. Dependency had become the characteristic of the laity."[2]

The restoration of the ministry of the laity is relatively new. Since the Reformation in the sixteenth century, the ministry of the laity has provided a growing dynamic in the life of the church, but there is a continuing struggle, particularly in the so-called mainline churches to work out a satisfactory relationship between the ministry of the clergy and the ministry of the laity. The organizational structures of the church and many theological seminaries tend to perpetuate a one-sided view of ministry which relates to the operation and maintenance of the local church or congregation. So long as both clergy and laity assume that the purpose of the church is the provision of a local worship centre, there is little incentive for a ministry of the laity, because the clergy are trained to organize that aspect of church life. On the other hand, when the local church is seen as the home base for the equipping of the people of God for their ministry in the world, then the whole picture changes and the New Testament concept of the church is restored: "Some to be apostles, some prophets, some evangelists, some pastors and teachers, to equip God's people for work in his service."[3] In other words, the service begins when the worship ends. However, since this involves a change in the self-image of many clergy and laity, it is natural that there should be resistance to the idea, and the impetus for change will probably have to come mainly from an enlightened laity.

William Diehl, a former manager of sales for the Bethlehem Steel Corporation and an enlightened and active layman in his church, has some strong words to say about "the gap between what the church proclaims as the role of Christian laypersons in the world and what the church actually does to support that role."

> In the almost thirty years of my professional career, my church has never once suggested that there be any type of accounting of my on-the-job ministry to others. My church has never once offered to improve those skills which could make me a better minister, nor was I ever asked if I needed any kind of support in what I was doing. There has never been an enquiry into the types of ethical decisions I must face, or whether I seek to communicate my faith to my co-workers. I have never been in a congregation where there was any type of public affirmation of a ministry in my career. In short, I must conclude that my church really doesn't have the least interest in whether or how I minister in my daily work.[4]

Although there are many congregations which are exceptions to Mr. Diehl's criticism, it is still generally true. I believe that the major reason for this neglect to equip and support the laity in their ministry in the workplace is that the majority of clergy is not trained for this task and coping with the pastoral needs of the congregation is usually a more than full-time ministry. The King-Bay Chaplaincy was established in 1977 in response to this particular need. It has been an experimental ministry designed to function as a research and development arm of the church, learning how to minister to the particular needs of the business community, and how to relate the gospel and Christian values to it.

The exercise of an effective ministry by lay people is largely a matter of self-confidence. Aware of our own shortcomings, we are inclined to say, "By what authority or power can I function as an ambassador for Christ where I live and work?" This is a natural response, and this is why it is important to return to our roots in the New Testament and discover that the church was built by ordinary people whose self-image was transformed by Christ, so that they could transform the world. Jesus, in calling his followers, probed not for their weakness, but for their strength and their potential was released; the apostle Saint Peter could later speak of the church as a "royal priesthood" of all believers empowered for ministry.

Mr. Diehl in analyzing the problem of liberating the laos from the church's built-in resistance to implementing the ministry of the laity concludes that,

> it must begin with the laity unlocking the doors of their own prisons of religious institutionalism and claiming their ministry in the world. It must be supported by professional church leaders who have caught the vision of God acting in today's world through the laity. Working together, the laos can thus shift the focus of the national church, its seminaries, districts, and congregations from seeing our religious institutions as ends in themselves to seeing them as a means to an end. The laos can and must be liberated for ministry in the world.[5]

Plausibility Structures

One of the major causes of the dependency of the laity on the clergy is the lack of what the Christian sociologist Peter Berger calls a "plausibility structure." The church itself is a plausibility structure, i.e., a social structure which validates belief. Berger says that there is no plausibility without an appropriate plausibility structure. So long as they remain and function within the structure of the institutional church, Christian laypeople have plausibility, but once they move into the secular structures of society and try to function as intentional Christians, it disappears. Perhaps this is why official pronouncements by church bodies on social issues appear to have so little effect. On the other hand Mother Teresa has great credibility when she speaks on compassion, because she has world-wide plausibility structure in her order of the Missionaries of Charity. The Salvation Army and inner city missions and the many Christian relief agencies have such structures. Most of these organizations are designed to serve the poor and needy, which is a generally accepted role for the church. But for Christianity in the workplace there is no plausibility structure and so ordinary lay people on the job lack a visible basis for their credibility.

The King-Bay Chaplaincy attempts to provide a plausibility structure within the business community. I believe we are having a measure of success, because many people, even those who are not actively involved in our programs, say to me, "Somehow it makes a difference to me, just knowing that the Chaplaincy is there. It is a reminder of the reality of the spiritual dimension in the midst of this totally secular environment."

Peter Berger points out that "world views remain firmly anchored in subjective certainty to the degree that they are supported by consistent and continuous plausibility structures."[6] The problem arises when we are caught up in competing loyalties to different world views. We all play many different, sometimes inconsistent roles in life. As a result we tend to maintain an inner detachment or distance with regard to some of these roles.

Hence there is a need for support groups and networks of various kinds to help the Christian maintain a faith perspective on the job. Encouraging signs indicate that such networks are forming in the workplace. There are a growing number of Christian professional organizations for scientists, engineers, lawyers, doctors, politicians, and unionized workers.

A Biblical Job Description for Lay Ministry

If the ministry of the church is to be faithful to the ministry of Christ, it must be essentially ministry to the world and that ministry must be done by those who work in the world. In 1977 a group of Roman Catholics issued the "Chicago Declaration of

Christian Concern" in which they stated that in the last analysis the church speaks to and acts upon the world through her laity. Without a dynamic laity conscious of its personal ministry to the world, the Church, in effect, does not speak or act. No amount of social actions by priests and religious leaders can ever be an adequate substitute for enhancing lay responsibility."

The ministry of the laity is the vocation or calling of every Christian to be a follower of Jesus Christ in daily life and work, and to continue his ministry to individuals and organizations. It is to be an ambassador, expressing the values of the kingdom of God through an intentional Christian lifestyle which reflects the individual's unique personality and gifts. (This concept of the intentional Christian lifestyle is developed in my book *It's Your Life, Create a Christian Lifestyle*.[7])

Those who work in the business community know the importance of a job description. Everyone needs some terms of reference and guidelines if he or she is to work harmoniously within an organization. In modern business the job description plus the corporate objectives provide the motivation and direction for management staff. The trend today is away from precisely defined job descriptions which can constrict and limit creative development. The idea is to make clear what the job is to accomplish within the given limits of responsibility, accountability, and authority. Along these lines it is possible to construct a biblical job description for lay ministry. As Saint Paul wrote, "Examine yourselves: are you living the life of faith? put yourselves to the test."[8]

What is the purpose of the job?

Jesus taught his followers to pray, "Thy kingdom come: thy will be done on earth as it is in heaven." In the Hebrew form of parallel expression, the second line amplifies and explains the first line. So "the Kingdom of Heaven is a society where God's will is as perfectly done on earth as it is in heaven. To be in the Kingdom of Heaven is to lead a life in which we have completely and willingly submitted everything to the will of God."[9]

In general terms, the Christian ideal in society would be a recognition of the sovereignty of God and the stewardship of man, in a community of love and peace. The onus is on each one of us to think through what the sovereignty of God, or lordship of Christ means in practical terms in our work situation, and to make sure that our decisions reflect a responsible stewardship of resources, and our human relations reflect the values of love, dignity, and respect for persons.

How is the job to be performed?
The key words of Jesus to those whom he called to be his disciples were, "Follow me." He called them to be with him, so that they could learn from him, be like him, think like him, and act like him. They were to be transformed in their thinking and values so that they could be God's agents for change, transforming the world.

Following Jesus is no simple matter; he was a very complex person whose ministry reflected the three key roles of prophet, priest, and king. If we are called to follow him, then in some way our ministry should reflect these roles.

1. The *role of the prophet* is not to predict the future, but to learn and make known the will of God to mankind, to call people to repentance in order to bring about the restoration of the kingdom of God. The followers of Jesus are to discern what is right in a given situation and to declare the will and the word of God.[10]

    This role is made difficult because our world has changed radically since biblical times. The corporation did not exist in Jesus' time, yet today it is the major force in our society for innovation, production, and marketing. It affects all of our lives. The problem is that church leaders have not addressed the reality of the corporations and our world. But it is the calling of the laity to work out this theological perspective with the guidance of the Holy Spirit.

2. The *role of the priest*, as one chosen by God and empowered by him, is to stand beside men and women and to lift them to God in prayerful concern. The priest is to be sensitive to the needs of people and minister to them. For a layperson, this is expressed mainly in one's attitude, not only to friends and relatives but to relationships in the workplace.

    The question is, How does a layperson function in a priestly way in the workplace? Regardless of one's position in an organization, the Christian attitude is to put people first, and to treat them with love, dignity, and respect, and to go beyond the utilitarian notion that the social responsibility of business is to increase its profits. The priestly business person puts "heart" into his business and provides a service to the community, not the least of which is the provision of jobs.

The King-Bay Chaplaincy responded to the unemployment crisis in 1983, when the recession was causing massive layoffs of business and professional men and women. These people, unlike the blue collar workers, had no support system such as the union, and very little in the way of appropriate government organization to help them cope with the trauma of prolonged unemployment. To meet this need, I was able to establish an organization called Operation Bootstrap designed to help this particular group of unemployed people to sort out their values and their life and career direction. With the latest in job-search and job-creation techniques, it has helped to rehabilitate and get over one thousand men and women back to work or to start new businesses of their own. The Bootstrap seminar and follow-up program is based upon spiritual values and principles, but it is open to people of all backgrounds and faiths and does not use theological language. Even so, one executive who went through the program wrote in the evaluation, "This has been the finest example of applied Christianity I have ever experienced."

The work of the royal priesthood relates not only to relief agencies for the poor and hungry, but also to the needs of the sophisticated and to the transformation of society by the application of the values of the kingdom of God.

3   The idea of following Jesus' *role as king* is probably quite foreign to most Christian people. After all, we are taught to be humble servants, and that doesn't quite fit the image we usually have of a king who represents pomp and circumstance and power. However, the biblical ideal of kingship is quite different. The king was a wise and compassionate ruler, who used his power to maintain order and freedom. The key characteristic of the king, as demonstrated by King Solomon, was to be a wise decison maker and manager.

Jesus accepted the reality of his kingship, but he transformed it into the style of a servant. He washed his disciples feet as an example of this paradoxical approach to leadership.

Servant leadership or kingship should not be mistaken for powerlessness or with allowing oneself to be used as a doormat. This misinterpretation has all too often given Christianity an image of weakness in the eyes of the world. Nothing happens without power. Perhaps the church would be more effective if Christian people could regain their confidence, reclaim their kingly, wise decision-making and leadership roles, not with arrogant coercion but with the enabling power of those who lead by example.

Job-Performance Evaluation

The Bible makes it clear that God expects faithful performance from his followers. " 'Well done, good and faithful servant!' said his master.'You have been faithful in managing small amounts, so I will put you in charge of large amounts. Come on in and share my happiness!' "[11] He also expects a very high quality of life: "So shall we all at last attain to the unity inherent in our faith and our knowledge of the Son of God — to mature personhood, measured by nothing less than the full stature of Christ."[12]

One of the basic principles of management is that responsibility, accountability, and authority are equally necessary for the satisfactory performance of any job. We must know the work for which we are responsible, we must know to whom we are accountable, and we must have the necessary authority to carry it out. For the ministry of the laity we have been given all three.

1. We are responsible for the development and use of the gifts we have been given. We are responsible as stewards for the good management of our time and resources. And we are responsible for sharing the gospel of Jesus Christ and for the extension of his kingdom on earth.[13]
2. We are accountable to God for our life and actions. This accountability is in proportion to the gifts and resources we have been given. "The man to whom much is given, of him much is required; the man to whom more is given, of him much more is required."[14]
3. Jesus taught as one having authority. He said, "I have been given all authority in heaven and on earth," and he has passed that authority on to his followers, "As the Father sent me, so I send you."[15]

Our Vocation and Gifts for Ministry

The psychologist Abraham Maslow, drawing on his observations of human behaviour, stated that "the only happy people I know are the ones who are working hard at something they consider is important," in other words, people who have some sense of vocation. Vocation is at the core of what one feels one must do with one's life.

Saint Paul writing to the Ephesians said, "I entreat you, then — as God has called you, live up to your vocation." Then he goes on to link vocation with gifts, "but each of us has been given his gift, his due portion of Christ's bounty."[16] We have all been given gifts and hence we all have a vocation or calling to follow Christ and to serve him in a particular ministry, reflecting our particular gifts.

One of the Reformation teachings regarding vocation, which has been neglected in the church, is the relationship between our Christian and our secular vocation. There has been a tendency to separate the two because, while many of the professions such as medicine or law can involve a strong sense of vocation, there are many jobs which provide a pay cheque but no sense of service. Yet I believe that we are called to offer whatever work we do to God, and to transform it in the process. The ideal would be a job which utilizes one's gifts, and in which the service provided could reflect a sense of ministry. In the course of leading Operation Bootstrap seminars for several hundred unemployed business men and women, I discovered a high percentage of people who, even in their fifties, had not yet decided what they wanted to be when they "grew up."

In the program we learned that the most effective way to arrive at a sense of life and career direction is first of all to clarify one's self-identity, one's gifts and strengths and one's sense of vocation. Then a personal profile is drawn which states, "This is who I am and the kind of person I am, this is what I enjoy doing and am good at, and this is what I feel called to do with my life." By the time one has sorted out these criteria, the life and career direction usually becomes clear.

There are two types of gifts in biblical teaching. The natural gifts are the God-given characteristics or traits with which we are born, such as a special ability in music or mathematics or art. To be good stewards of these abilities we need to discover and develop them with practice and hard work. The other type are the special gifts of the Holy Spirit, known as grace gifts or charismatic gifts. They are distributed within a congregation to empower or enable it to function as the body of Christ and to manifest the kingdom of God. These gifts are not given to confer some special or superior status upon those who receive them; they are intended as the power tools of the church, to be handled with great care and humility to enhance the life of the church."And these were his gifts: some to be apostles, some prophets, some evangelists, some pastors and teachers, to equip God's people for work in his service, to the building up of the body of Christ."[17]

A congregation cannot be mature if it has only a few outstanding leaders who exercise charisma. The diversity of gifts available within the Christian community need to be discovered and used. Because many people do not feel that they have any gifts or talents to offer, a primary task of the church is to help us discover our gifts and, in spite of our doubts and fears, to hold us accountable for them so that we can enter into the joy of creating.

The parable of the talents reminds us that it is not important how many talents we have, one or five. If they are used, our lives will expand and our capacity will double. If they are not used, they atrophy and the self is diminished. (I have included in Appendix 15 a simple questionnaire designed to facilitate the identification of personal gifts. It is most helpful when used in groups who know each other well enough to be aware of each other's gifts.)

Ministry and Personality

God has not only created us with a variety of gifts for life and ministry, he has also created a wide variety of personality types, each with a particular way of relating to people, ideas, and things. We each have innate preferences which make us more suited to some types of occupations and ministries than others.

Hence a knowledge of one's particular personality profile is not only a helpful guide in the difficult process of choosing a career but also provides an indication of the type of Christian lay ministry for which we are best suited.

The psychologist Carl Jung discovered and categorized the basic life preferences which combine in different ways to shape our personality. Others have developed tests based on Jung's work, such as the Myers-Briggs Type Indicator, which accurately reflect personality characteristics and behavioural preferences; in most cases this proves to be an exciting process of self-discovery.

When these tests were related to the key biblical characters, it was discovered, for example, that each of the four gospel writers represented a different personality type and hence brought a different perspective to the accounts of Jesus' life and ministry. It has also been discovered that different approaches to prayer and personal spiritual growth are suited to the different personality types. For example, some people who find prayer difficult are simply using a method which is not suited to their personality type.

Space does not permit further enlargement on this topic in this book, but for those who want to learn more about it I commend to you the books I have listed in the Bibliography under Ministry and Personality.

The Power of Images

When we have a sense of our vocation and have identified our gifts for ministry, we face the question, How do I actually translate my faith into practical action? I believe the key lies in value-based decision making. Values come together to form images, and images shape our lives. Each of us has a number of self-images that give meaning to our experiences. Sometimes they are in conflict. Consciously or unconsciously we select images of the sort of person we would like to become, and these images motivate us toward life goals, and influence our choices and decisions. Sooner or later, we settle on a master image as the dominant one to guide our life journey.

A Christian is a person who guides his or her life not by church doctrine but by a central biblical image. Doctrines only shape our lives when they become images, and we tend to get our images through verbal pictures. That is why Jesus taught in stories and parables. His ministry was shaped by his image of the kingdom of God, and he intended that image to be central for his followers.

Jesus went through a struggle in the wilderness sorting out his own self-image; should he be a miracle worker, feed the hungry, or use political power? He rejected each image and chose to be the suffering servant of God who could say to his followers, "I am the way, the truth and the life."

The most practical way for Christians to respond when faced with difficult decisions in our complex world is to prayerfully ask, What would Jesus do in this situation? This will only be effective if we are able to develop an accurate biblical picture of Jesus in contemporary terms. Can we visualize Jesus in a business suit or overalls? Can we cultivate his perspective, values, and way of thinking? A tall order, but that is what is expected of us, "Let this mind be in you, which was also in Christ Jesus."[18] To assist those who want to work on cultivating the "mind of Christ," I have included in Appendix 16 an exercise which has been found helpful in groups as they try to reach a consensus on what Jesus' attitude would be towards a number of contemporary questions.

Questions for Personal Reflection or Group Discussion

1. What are some of the ways in which the local church could be more supportive of the ministry of the laity in the workplace?
2. Do you agree that acceptance of the ministry of the laity will most likely be the result of an awakened laity giving leadership in church circles? What part can you play in this process?
3. As a personal exercise, write your own job description for your ministry, using the biblical job description as a guide.
4. Form a group of people who want to grow together and use the material on vocation and gifts to clarify your own basis for ministry in the workplace.
5. Use the form in Appendix 15 on The Mind of Christ with a group to clarify your own image of Jesus in contemporary terms.

10
A Strategy for Lay Ministry

One thing you must see to whatever happens — live a life that is worthy of a citizen of the kingdom of God and of the Gospel of Christ. . . . Stand fast, united in one spirit, fighting with a single mind for the faith of the Gospel. Philippians 1:27-28

The community of faith has a vocation as a counter cultural community and not as a mirror of society, for it is called to give witness through word and deed to an alternative to life as it is. John Westerhoff

The Local Church and Lay Ministry

In order to live lives that are worthy of citizens of the kingdom of God, we must first have a vision of the kingdom on earth. Then in faith we may hope that the vision is achievable and that God will supply the power to enable us to make it happen.

In the previous chapters we have considered some practical ways and means of applying our faith in the workplace and in the business community in particular. We reflected upon our world in transition and shared a vision of the unshakable kingdom of God and the ideal of *shalom:* life characterized by well-being, peace, liberation, justice, and whole community. We are called to live for this vision. It is my hope that my suggestions for lay ministry will be found helpful by individuals and groups of men and women who have a vison of exercising a ministry in their daily life and work. Christianity is not an individual affair; it is essentially the life of a community expressed through individuals, who through baptism have been incorporated into the body of Christ. The church is the continuing manifestation of the people of God in the world. As such, the ministry of the laity can never be divorced from the life and worship of the local church. Unfortunately the connection between the two is often hard to find.

John Westerhoff says that, "we need to ask to what extent our rituals, our experiences in the community of faith, and our action in the world express God's vision for humanity. Our society, the church included, is largely without visions, which means without clear and adequate goals."[1]

God has given us the vision of his kingdom and *shalom* as its quality of life. When the local church loses sight of this vision it begins to die. There is no motivation for lay mission and ministry and its life becomes a dull routine of religious duty. A sure formula for a dead church is an over-active clergyman and a passive laity. There is no sense of the excitement which comes from being actively involved as God's agents for change in the world. There are no personal stories to tell of successes and failures on the front line. People, particularly young people, need a vision in which to invest their lives. Without it, church-going can degenerate into an assessment of the performance of the minister and the choir.

On the other hand, the dynamic and growing churches are those which inspire their members to accept the challenge of lay ministry and support them in their vocations. In any congregation which is open to the leading of his Spirit, God provides a variety of special gifts and ministries, "to equip God's people for work in his service," which results in "the building up of the body of Christ."[2] Christ's ministry was in and to the world, and the aim of every congregation should be to become a ministering community. "The church's task is to help people discern and witness to the presence of God in the midst of life, to see the ultimate meaning in and beyond the immediate meaning of any given human enterprise."[3] If the objective of Christian education and preaching is merely to produce better-informed Christians, the motivation to learn is minimal. But if there is a vision of being used by God to help build a better world through applied Christianity, a new dynamic flows into the congregation and the power for ministry is released.

If the church is serious about lay ministry it will revise its liturgies to include greater participation by lay people. Not only in the traditional aspects of worship, but it will develop ways of recognizing, honouring, and celebrating the secular occupations through which its members are exercising their ministries. The word *liturgy* literally means "the work of the people," and the gap between the church and the world identified in Chapter 1 will begin to be closed when daily work and Sunday worship are integrated in a meaningful way. The Celtic church of Saint Columba of Iona taught and demonstrated that "to pray is to work and to work is to pray." They taught better methods of fishing and farming as they preached the gospel.

One way in which the local church can recognize the ministry of the laity is to provide a form of commissioning lay people to ministry in their particular occupation or profession. A very active Christian, who was a pilot with a major airline, was commissioned in this way. Over a period of time he was able to bring a new spirit of mutual caring and concern among the flight crews and Pilots' Association, which resulted in the introduction of an Employee Assistance Program by the company. This ensures that employees with problems which affect their work performance are given appropriate help to deal with their situation. A sample of a commissioning service for lay ministry is included in Appendix 17.

Adult Education

Adult education or androgogy is different from the education of children (pedagogy). A child needs to feed the memory banks of the brain with information, and to be trained in how to think and use information. Without a foundation of basic knowledge in the various disciplines such as mathematics and language, it is not possible to grow and function intelligently. However, adults usually have the basics; they have acquired an enormous amount of information by observation and experience. Their primary need is to learn how to apply the information to achieve their own objectives. Motivation is the key to their learning; they learn what they need to know in order to do what they want to do. Thus, training in the use of a problem-solving process such as the one described in Chapter 8, plus access to relevant information, is one of the most effective forms of adult education and lay training.

In my experience, a high percentage of Christians feel that they have a very inadequate knowledge of the Bible, and this inhibits a confident approach to lay ministry. It would take many years of personal and group Bible study to achieve competence and I believe that this is the rock upon which many lay training programs founder. They usually attempt to give lay people a condensed version of the kind of education given to clergy in seminary. Church history, theology, philosophy of religion, biblical hermeneutics are necessary for a professional religious calling but may not be the most practical and useful information for a lay ministry.

It is far more practical, as the cliché has it, to teach a person how to fish than to stuff him with fish when he is hungry. In other words, instead of giving people endless religious information which they may never use, give them a vision of what God is calling them to do with their lives. Then train them in the full problem-solving process, from scanning the situation in the light of kingdom ideals, to analyzing situations, setting objectives, finding creative solutions, and planning for action. Provide them with information resources and they will learn what they need to know in order to do what they want to do.

With this approach people will not experience the discouragement of trying to digest the whole Bible before they can function as confident Christians in the world. They do need to learn what kind of book it is and how to use it as their central resource library. After all, the Bible is a conveniently bound library of sixty-six different kinds of books containing history, theology, poetry, values, ethics, spiritual guidance, and inspiration. The key to knowledge today is not just a good memory, but the intelligence to ask the right questions and a good retrieval system to find the data by which answers can be developed. Such books as the *Thompson Chain Reference Bible*, which contains an extensive topical index, is much more useful than a concordance, which requires an initial knowledge of the content and the language used in a particular version of the Bible. It is now possible to use a home computer to store biblical passages arranged on a topical basis for easy access. So, for example, one can have an instant printout on everything Jesus or Paul had to say about any topic.

Doing Theology

One of the essential skills for lay ministry is learning how to "theologize" or to think theologically. To me this means learning how to make sense out of everyday life and its problems from a biblical or kingdom perspective. What are the questions of our time? What are the root causes of our problems? Remember how Jesus went to the bottom of the family quarrel over inheritance? What biblical values apply, and in the light of these values, what do you think would be the "word of the Lord" in this situation? This is doing theology.

There are many ways to approach this process, but I believe that spiritual value clarification, as described in Chapter 3, is the most direct and relevant way (including such exercises as the one on discerning the mind of Christ in Appendix 16).

The Context for Lay Training

The most common form of lay training tends to be related to the needs of the local congregation. This includes how to teach Sunday school, lead a group, raise money, sing in the choir, and visit the sick. These functions are necessary for the life of the local Christian community and logically the training takes place in the local church. However, when we consider training for ministry in society and in the workplace, other factors need to be considered. A pluralistic society is not structured on denominational lines, and in my experience in the business ministry, denominational labels are either irrelevant or a hinderance. I do not believe, for example, that a business or workplace chaplaincy would be acceptable on any basis other than ecumenical or non-denominational. The urge to wave denominational flags comes from the church institution, not the individuals who are trying to apply their faith on the job.

Christian Networks

The major problem for the Christian in the workplace is isolation and the sense of being alone in the totally secular work environment. In our business chaplaincy, our lunch-hour groups are composed of men and women of all denominational backgrounds; they simply accept each other as fellow Christians, and there is usually a sense of relief at not having to hide behind denominational barriers. This is the networking phenomenon of our time. Dr. Lyle Schaller, a church-management consultant with a wide knowledge of the church in both Canada and the United States, says that wherever he goes, he finds a spreading network of small groups of Christians. They are getting together in every imaginable setting to study, discuss, and pray together, and to support each other in the difficult task of living the faith in the workplace. Through our quarterly Chaplaincy newsletter we link together a network of over 1,300 people in business, industry, government, and labour. The potential for the influence of these networks is great.

The question is, How should the institutional church relate to these free-floating ecumenical groups? Perhaps this is God's answer to the scandal of the divided church. The workplace is the front line of the mission of the church in modern society, and we do not have to wait for the unlikely reunion of all the churches before we can co-operate in a significant way on the front line. Such co-operation is no threat to individual denominational affiliation. Many lapsed Christians have been reactivated and returned to their denominational roots; very few have found any reason to change their affiliation. On the other hand, the diversity has provided a richness to the group life.

The most constructive way in which the local church can relate to the ecumenical network is to see it as a movement of the Spirit, and to encourage the members to get involved without any sense of guilt or disloyalty to their denomination. Far from detracting from the life of the local church, those who have an active lay ministry and ecumenical support group, tend to bring a freshness and vitality into the local church, particularly if it is oriented towards lay ministry.

In addition to the informal networks, there are a growing number of Christian professional organizations for doctors, nurses, lawyers, business people. In all of these groups new educational and training contexts will have to be developed, if they are to have the depth and competence needed to relate Christian values and the gospel to our complex society. The type of training and curriculum will have to be quite different from that which is usually offered in the local church.

The King-Bay Chaplaincy, in its research and development capacity, has been experimenting with various forms of lay training. We have found that evening courses which start shortly after work and finish early, as well as more intensive weekend seminars in a residential setting, get the best response. The courses usually run one evening a week for six weeks. These are held in seminar facilities in the office towers. Some courses are also being sponsored in co-operation with a large city-based community college.

We follow a two-year cycle in which we cover various aspects of the following major themes:

— lay ministry in the workplace
— theology in the workplace
— Christianity and social issues
— management from a Christian perspective
— business ethics
— lifestyle/workstyle/leadership style
— work and technology

The leadership of the seminars is mainly drawn from the business and educational communities.

Ministry in the Workplace

In the previous chapters we have considered in some detail what I believe are some of the major areas of concern for lay ministry, and some practical methods of approach. To sum up and provide a convenient way of applying these ideas in a practical way, I have organized the following review around two aspects of lay ministry: personal preparation, the journey inward, and active involvement, the journey outward.

The Journey Inward

1 Develop self-knowledge
Self-knowledge and self-understanding is the beginning of the process. Begin with yourself: a gifted child of God; a person with

particular gifts to be developed and used for ministry and service; a person with a special sense of vocation or calling; a follower of Jesus, with a mandate to continue his ministry on earth and committed to putting the kingdom of God first in your life. Every decision you make stems from your sense of self-identity, and your relationship with God. When the apostles Peter and John were on trial before the Jewish Sanhedrin, people were amazed at the boldness of these untrained laymen in witnessing to the power of Jesus. Then they noticed that these men had been with Jesus. If our ministry is to be effective people must notice the same thing about us. We cultivate the mind of Christ by meditating upon his life and teaching. And we express the love of Christ in an intentional Christian lifestyle and workstyle. This is the foundation; without it we lack integrity.

2 Develop a Christian perspective
Develop a clear Christian value system, centering on loving relationships and a responsible stewardship attitude to all of life. This will form a basis for your decisions and choices.

3 Develop discipline
Practice a personal discipline for the maintenance and growth of your own spiritual life through worship, prayer, study, and group fellowship.

4 Develop the servant leadership style
Cultivate the enabling-servant leadership style of Jesus. This is based on the understanding that enabling others to reach their potential is the most effective form of management or leadership today.

5 Discover your gifts
Discover and affirm your gifts and vocation, and apply them in your present work situation. Develop a vision of the way things should be in your workplace from a Christian perspective, and work out a strategy for change.

Moral Courage in the Workplace
It is not easy to go against the stream. The desire to conform, to be identified with a particular group, is very strong in all of

us because we want to be accepted and to belong. The way we dress, where we live, the car we drive, all tend to say where we fit into society. There is nothing wrong with a certain amount of outward conformity to our social group. However, scripture has some strong words about the danger of inner conformity. "Adapt yourselves no longer to the pattern of this present world, but let your minds be remade and your whole nature thus transformed. Then you will be able to discern the will of God, and to know what is good, acceptable and perfect."[4] God's word goes beyond outward appearance to the inner world of our values, attitudes, and beliefs, which together shape our conscience. When we really get to know Jesus, our conscience comes alive with a sensitivity we never dreamed possible.

The question is, how do we resist the pressure to conform in the workplace, especially when we have a career in which we want to advance? What do we do when our boss asks us to do something that goes against our conscience as a Christian? If the issue is serious enough, we may have to put our job on the line. But in most cases the issue can be tactfully worked through, and we can then take the long-term route of trying to bring about a change in the policy concerned. However we go about it, it takes moral courage to be a representative of the kingdom of God in the workplace. We don't have to be pious or holier-than-thou about it, but there will be times when we must uphold certain values and put people before profit.

The Journey Outward

Our mission is to actualize or make real the kingdom of God where we live and work. "The people of God cannot rest until the values of the city of God have become the values of the city of man."[5]

1 Develop a vision
The art of management by objective is to be able to visualize the desired end result so clearly that planning and action follow as a natural process. If we don't have a clear vision of the way we would like things to be, we are likely to drift along with a vague feeling of discontent with the way things are. It is essential that

we develop a vision of how things would be in our workplace if the values of the kingdom of God were operative in that situation.

Perhaps we need some modern analogies such as Jesus used when he said the kingdom of God is like the tiny mustard seed, a small beginning with a large result; it is like yeast, which when mixed with the flour, leavens the whole loaf; it is like treasure or the pearl of great price, for which one would sell everything. It will always meet with a mixed reaction like seeds falling on different types of soil. In today's terms it might be like having a job in which one can grow and fulfil one's potential, or like working in a caring and co-operative community of people. It is like having a boss who is always fair and just in his dealings and treats people with love, dignity, and respect.

Unless we can visualize it, we are not likely to make it happen. Modern athletes in training have discovered the secret of visualization. They mentally prepare themselves before the ski run, or the skating routine, or the high jump, by mentally picturing themselves actually going through the process. Can we think through and visualize ourselves dealing with our work problems and business decisions from a Christian value perspective? (See Appendix 18 for suggested guidelines for an appropriate Christian lifestyle).

2 Develop a plan of action

Nothing much happens until we plan to make it happen. This is where we use the creative problem-solving process introduced in Chapter 8. The process begins with an analysis of the situation to determine the need or problem. We must stand back and reflect upon what is happening in our workplace. How are people treated? Is the atmosphere hostile or caring? How are decisions made? What values lie behind the behaviour? The next step is diagnosis. Why are things the way they are? (Until we know the cause of the problem we cannot solve it).

At this point we have to decide how we are going to respond to the situation. We can decide to go with the stream, keep our point of view to ourselves, and avoid the issue; we can adapt and accommodate to the situation; or we can decide to be change agents for God. If we choose the latter, what needs to be changed?

What is our objective? And how are we going to bring about the change? We look for support among those who share our values and develop our plan of action and carry it out.

3 Develop a ministry to the spirit of your organization

The church has traditionally ministered to the spirit of individuals. I believe it is equally important that we learn how to minister to the spirit of organizations and corporations, because as William Stringfellow points out, organizations are often the form that the "principalities and powers" take in our society. Negative forces sometimes operate in a manner which does not appear to be under the control of individuals in the system.

In Chapter 4 we explored in some detail the ways in which we can exercise a ministry to the spirit of the organization in which we work. It is now recognized that this spirit is one of the major factors in determining the success or failure of a company. Research into the dynamics of the most successful companies indicates that those which operate on the basis of values which put people first are the most successful. In other words, the values of the kingdom of God are practical, and when properly applied they work better than traditional workplace values. The implications of this for the rediscovery of the relevance of Christianity are enormous. They provide a new framework for thinking about the ministry of the laity.

I believe that it is possible for a few people, with a clear vision, to bring about significant change in an organization over a period of time. It is clear that some organizations are spiritually sick and their future is in jeopardy. Just as the doctor uses his stethoscope to listen for signs of trouble in the human body, or the pastor listens to the troubles of the individual he is counselling, so the Christian layperson can develop a sensitivity to the signs of sickness in his organization.

Bob is a vice-president in a major brokerage firm. When a member of his family died, he expected the company to demonstrate its concern by having a company representative attend the funeral. When no one came from the company, Bob was not particularly concerned about himself, but he reflected how this would affect other employees who might not have family support. He felt that some important spiritual values were at stake; so he raised the issue with the regional president of the company, who took the matter seriously and an employee assistance program has been introduced and will provide a counselling service related to personal and health concerns. Bob does not parade his Christianity, but it is generally known that he is an active churchman. When people see kingdom values applied in a practical way to humanize the work environment, I believe it will begin to restore the credibility and attractiveness of Christianity in the workplace.

4 Build a sense of community in the workplace
As we saw in Chapter 6 a most effective form of ministry in a company is to build a sense of co-opeative community among the employees. This has been one of the keys to the success of Japanese business and industry. Our system has largely been based on competitive individualism, which tends to destroy trust and the co-operation essential for a productive workforce.

Frank was hired as the comptroller of a large law firm. When he started work, he soon discovered what might be called a bad spirit in the office. Everyone seemed to be so driven by the need to produce, that there was little time to be human. The lawyers had to keep the computer informed of every minute they spent on each client's account, and they tended to treat the secretaries as machines to handle the typing load. There was no sense of community, and it was a very unpleasant place to work.

Frank sized up the situation and decided to try to change it. He began by treating the secretaries with dignity and respect; he showed an interest in them as persons. Soon a new atmosphere of care and co-operation developed; the lawyers learned to relax a bit. Gradually the work environment changed, and it became a happy place to work. Frank might not use the term, but he was exercising a valuable ministry.

5 The prophetic ministry
This aspect of lay ministry is being introduced here because it belongs to a mature stage of the journey outward. Until by example and humility we have developed credibility and acceptance within the organization, it is unwise and probably counter-productive to assume a prophetic role. However, in time it may

be appropriate and necessary to take the risk of speaking out against injustice, wrongdoing, poor stewardship, or bad management. The political columnist Dalton Camp, in an article in the *Toronto Star* entitled "Business Should Brush Up on Ethics," lists a number of major corporations which have been convicted by the courts of ethical wrongdoing. A major electronics firm filed 108 false expense claims on a defence contract. A highly respectable brokerage house "was found to be regularly depositing bogus cheques, amounting to some $10 billion a day, in a number of unsuspecting banks and pocketing the undeserved interest therefrom."[6] In the same week a former defence secretary went to jail for lying about an insider stock deal. Dalton Camp goes on to say, "The impression is inescapable, while watching one or another uneasy senior spokesperson appearing on television for a troubled corporation, that an ethical vacuum does exist in corporate affairs, that there is a bleak unfamiliarity with concepts of right and wrong simply because such words never come up back at the office."[7]

Clearly there is as great a need for a prophetic voice in the workplace today as there was when the prophet Amos proclaimed the word of the Lord. "For crime after crime of Israel I will grant them no reprieve, because they sell the innocent for silver and the destitute for a pair of shoes. They grind the heads for the poor into the earth and thrust the humble out of their way."[8] However, there is a risk involved; prophets are never popular and frequently suffer at the hands of the vested interests that they disturb. It is also very difficult sometimes to sort out what is the right thing to do in the complex and interrelated issues of our time, but that does not excuse us from exercising moral power in the face of political and economic power. It is an abdication of moral responsibility to say that the business person is simply required to look after the interests of the shareholders and to maximize profits.

6 Personal witness

In some ways this is the most difficult aspect of ministry in the workplace because it is the most personal. As part of my doctoral studies on values in the business community I discovered that although the majority felt that their religious beliefs were relevant to their work situation, sixty-six per cent felt that their beliefs were largely a private matter. Only thirty-four per cent saw their faith as having public or corpoate application. The idea of sharing one's faith in the lordship of Christ is very difficult for most people, and the pluralistic nature of the workplace makes it even more inhibiting. It is easy to say I will witness to my faith by my example, and most of the time this is the appropriate course of action. However, there are times when we should be able to give a reason for the hope that is in us, and do it with modesty and respect. To witness, of course, does not mean preaching or moralizing; it simply means sharing something of what God means to you, and how he has acted in your life.

Secular Saints
The saints were not stained-glass window images of perfection. They were the ordinary faithful followers of Jesus. We are all called to be this kind of saint, but it is not easy in the work environment where the name of Jesus is more likely to be used in profanity than adoration. It takes moral courage, and for that we need the moral support of other Christians. Therefore, the first priority for anyone who determines to be an ambassador for Christ in the workplace is to find or form a Christian support group. Unfortunately it is often hard to identify the Christians in an organization, because most prefer to keep a very low profile. However, if you keep your antennae out, you are sure to find someone in the company who shares a common faith in Christ, even though he or she might wear a different denominational hat. Begin by meeting weekly for lunch. Use the networking concept and you will soon be joined by others. Then your group can determine how it wants to function. When the group is settled, use the grapevine to find other groups, and link up with them to form a network of support and influence. Then plan occasional larger gatherings. Thus the Christian community becomes a visible reality in the workplace, a manifestation of the kingdom, because the King who promised that, whenever two or three gather in his name, is there in the midst.

With the support of your group you can begin to consider how to exercise your faith on the job. Do a problem/opportunity scan of your work situation and find where your Christian values need to be applied, (see Appendix 12) and then use the problem-solving process to develop a plan and work at it with sensitive understanding. See your desk or workbench as an altar, and you will find a ministry that is as acceptable to God as any ordained ministry. The best model I can think of is the well-known seventeenth-century monk, brother Lawrence, who felt as close to God as he was doing the dishes in the monastry kitchen as he did in church. Among his many letters of spiritual guidance he wrote these words.

> It is not necessary for being with God to be always in church. We may make an oratory of our heart wherein to retire from time to time to converse with him in meekness, humility and love. Everyone is capable of such familiar conversation with God, some more, some less. . . . He requires no great matters of us: a little remembrance of him from time to time, a little adoration, sometimes to pray for his grace, sometimes to offer him your sufferings, and sometimes to return him thanks for the favors he has given you, and still gives you in the midst of your troubles, and to console yourself with him the oftenest you can. Lift up your heart to him, sometimes even at your meals, and when you are in company: the least little remembrance will always be acceptable to him. You need not cry very loud, he is nearer to us than we are aware of. Accustom yourself, then, by degrees thus to worship him, to beg his grace, to offer him your heart from time to time in the midst of your business, even every moment if you can. . . . He knows what we can do. Let us begin then.[9]

Questions for Personal Reflection or Group Discussion

1 Does your local church function as an outpost of the kingdom of God in the community? What do you think would be marks of that kind of church?
2 In your church is there a strong sense of the importance of the mission and ministry of the laity in the world? In what ways could the local church strengthen and support your ministry

in the workplace? It may be helpful to use the problem-solving process which begins by considering the gap between the ideal and the actual.
3 How would you develop an educational program for adults who want to express their faith in the workplace? (See the Bibliography at the end of the Appendix.)
4 Use the five points listed under the Journey Inward and the six points under the Journey Outward as a checklist for becoming more intentional about your Christian life and ministry.

Appendix 1
The King-Bay Chaplaincy

In October 1977 the King-Bay Chaplaincy was established by the Rev. Dr. Graham Tucker and his secretary Mrs. Ruth Cartwright at the invitation of a group of business people, who felt that there was a need for an identifiable Christian ministry in the heart of the Toronto business district. A board of directors representing the major denominations was established and the organization was incorporated as an ecumenical ministry.

The purpose of the Chaplaincy is:

To *gather* Christian businessmen and women for mutual support, encouragement and study in a network of small groups.

To *equip* people for lay ministry in the workplace, through educational programs.

To *serve* the needs of individuals seeking healing and wholeness in personal and corporate life, through counselling and seminars.

To *influence* business to apply Christian principles and values which further the kingdom of God in the workplace, through conferences, seminars, and consulting.

To establish a positive *connection* between the churches and the workplace.

The Chaplaincy functions as a research and development arm of the churches, dedicated to bridging the gap between the institutional church and the workplace. The insights gained are shared through a quarterly newsletter. Most of the insights in this book are the outcome of the Chaplaincy ministry.

One of the achievements of the Chaplaincy was the establishment of Operation Bootstrap, an organization which in the past four years has helped over 1,300 unemployed business people to find or create jobs.

Appendix 2
Magna's Corporate Constitution

Board of Directors
Magna believes that outside directors provide independent counsel and discipline. A majority of Magna's Board of Directors will be outsiders.

Employee Equity and Profit Participation
Ten per cent of Magna's profit before tax will be allocated to employees. These funds will be used for the purchase of Magna shares in trust for employees and for cash distributions to employees, recognizing both performance and length of service.

Shareholder Profit Participation
Magna will distribute, on average, 20 per cent of its annual net profit to its shareholders.

Management Profit Participation
In order to obtain a long term contractual commitment from management, the Company provides a compensation arrangement which, in addition to a base salary comparable to industry standards, allows for the distribution to corporate management of up to 6 per cent of Magna's profit before tax.

Research and Technology Development
Magna will allocate 7 per cent of its profit before tax for research and technology development to ensure the long term viability of the Company.

Social Responsibility
The company will contribute 2 per cent of its profit before tax to charitable, cultural, educational and political institutions to support the basic fabric of society.

Minimum Profit Performance
Management has an obligation to produce a profit. If Magna does not generate a minimum after-tax return of 4 per cent on share capital for two consecutive years, Class A shareholders, voting as a Class, will have the right to elect additional directors.

Major Investments
In the event that more than 20 per cent of Magna's equity is to be committed to a new unrelated business, Class A and Class B shareholders will have the right to approve such an investment with each class voting separately.

Constitutional Amendments
Any change to Magna's Corporate Constitution will require the approval of the Class A and Class B shareholders with each class voting separately.

Appendix 3
Our Commitment to You

As an employee of one of the Magna International companies we would like to keep you informed about your rights and responsibilities and about the way we operate.

Magna is committed to an operating philosophy which is based on fairness and concern for people. It includes these principles:

- Magna believes that every employee should own a portion of the company — to find out how you are a shareholder, ask your General Manager for the booklet on Employee Equity Participation and Profit Sharing.
- We are committed to improving wages and benefits as we improve productivity through advanced technology.
- We feel that job security is very important and we will make every effort to protect it.
- We will ensure that working conditions are pleasant and safe. If at any time you notice that equipment or conditions are unsafe, let your Safety Committee know; if things don't improve, call the Corporate Human Resources Department.
- We want you to be treated fairly — and if at any time you feel that you are not treated this way or that you are being discriminated against, call the Corporate Human Resources Department.

If you feel that these principles are not being followed, and you believe that you cannot get the situation corrected, the Corporate Human Resources Department wants to know about it.

Call the direct line (416) 477-6823 or write to: 36 Apple Creek Blvd., Markham, Ontario L3R 4Y4. Attn.: Corporate Human Resources Department.

Appendix 4
A Business Creed for Corporate Excellence

- *We Believe* that Corporate Excellence depends upon the development of a vital "spirit" or esprit de corps in the organization.
- *We Believe* that the "spirit" or culture of the company reflects the vision, values and philosophy of its senior management.
- *We Believe* that the most successful corporations knowingly or unknowingly follow spiritually based operating principles.
- *We Believe* that a positive corporate Identity or Image, held by both the public and the employees, is an essential basis for corporate excellence.
- *We Believe* that the value system of an organization must be ethically sound, understood and accepted by all members of the organization.
- *We Believe* that the people in an organization are its greatest resource and most valuable asset.
- *We Believe* in the essential equality, dignity and worth of the individual but recognize differences in ability, capacity and competence.
- *We Believe* that the success of a corporation is a responsibility shared by both workers and management.
- *We Believe* that the work is as important to the worker as the worker is to the work.
- *We Believe* in honourably earned profits.

- *We Believe* that a just and equitable balance must be maintained between the rights and well-being of the employees and rights and well-being of the organization.
- *We Believe* in a co-operative approach to labour-management relations based on trust and open communication.
- *We Believe* that a strong sense of community and mutual caring between the company and the employees is the most effective basis for loyalty and high productivity.
- *We Believe* in a participatory and enabling management style which inspires commitment.
- *We Believe* that technology should be the servant not the master of man.
- *We Believe* in the stewardship or responsible management of the environment and material and technical resources of the world.

(Developed by the King-Bay Chaplaincy)

Appendix 5
Value-Analysis Profile 1

Corporate Purpose or Mission

1.01 The purpose or mission of our organization is unclear to management.

Presently
0 1 2 3 4 5 6 7 8 9
+-+-+-+-+-+-+-+-+-+
0 1 2 3 4 5 6 7 8 9
Ideally

The purpose or organization is clear to management.

1.02 The purpose or mission of our organization is unclear to those below the management level.

Presently
0 1 2 3 4 5 6 7 8 9
+-+-+-+-+-+-+-+-+-+
0 1 2 3 4 5 6 7 8 9
Ideally

The purpose or mission of our organization is clear to those below the management level.

1.03 Our organization's purpose does not motivate me to be creative or committed to high productivity.

Presently
0 1 2 3 4 5 6 7 8 9
+-+-+-+-+-+-+-+-+-+
0 1 2 3 4 5 6 7 8 9
Ideally

Our organization's purpose motivates me to be creative and committed to productivity.

1.04 Our organization's purpose is neither upheld nor communicated effectively.

Presently
0 1 2 3 4 5 6 7 8 9
+-+-+-+-+-+-+-+-+-+
0 1 2 3 4 5 6 7 8 9
Ideally

Our organization's purpose is constantly held up and communicated to all employees.

Appendices 169

1.05 The success of our organization is only measured by the size of its profit.

Presently
0 1 2 3 4 5 6 7 8 9
+-+-+-+-+-+-+-+-+-+
0 1 2 3 4 5 6 7 8 9
Ideally

The success of our organization is measured by its service to society as well as its profit.

1.06 Our organization exists primarily for the benefit of the owners (stakeholders).

Presently
0 1 2 3 4 5 6 7 8 9
+-+-+-+-+-+-+-+-+-+
0 1 2 3 4 5 6 7 8 9
Ideally

Our organization exists for the benefit of both the owners (stakeholders) and the employees.

1.07 In our organization management authority is based on the rights of owners and shareholders.

Presently
0 1 2 3 4 5 6 7 8 9
+-+-+-+-+-+-+-+-+-+
0 1 2 3 4 5 6 7 8 9
Ideally

Management authority is based on the loyalty and commitment of those who work in the organization.

1.08 Employees feel little sense of loyalty and commitment to the organization.

Presently
0 1 2 3 4 5 6 7 8 9
+-+-+-+-+-+-+-+-+-+
0 1 2 3 4 5 6 7 8 9
Ideally

Employees are highly committed and loyal to the organization.

1.09 Management has a primary responsibility to those who provide the capital for the organization.

Presently
0 1 2 3 4 5 6 7 8 9
+-+-+-+-+-+-+-+-+-+
0 1 2 3 4 5 6 7 8 9
Ideally

Management has an equal responsibility towards those who provide its labour and its capital.

Value-Analysis Profile 2

Corporate Sense of Identity

2.01 The organization's name is not well known in the community.
Presently
0 1 2 3 4 5 6 7 8 9
+-+-+-+-+-+-+-+-+-+
0 1 2 3 4 5 6 7 8 9
Ideally
The organization's name is widely known in the community.

2.02 The organization's name does not convey a clear image of the business we are in.
Presently
0 1 2 3 4 5 6 7 8 9
+-+-+-+-+-+-+-+-+-+
0 1 2 3 4 5 6 7 8 9
Ideally
The organization's name is instantly recognized and associated with our line of business.

2.03 The public image of the organization is negative.
Presently
0 1 2 3 4 5 6 7 8 9
+-+-+-+-+-+-+-+-+-+
0 1 2 3 4 5 6 7 8 9
Ideally
The public image of the organization is positive.

2.04 The average employee is not proud to be working for the organization.
Presently
0 1 2 3 4 5 6 7 8 9
+-+-+-+-+-+-+-+-+-+
0 1 2 3 4 5 6 7 8 9
Ideally
The average employee is proud to be associated with the organization.

2.05 The organization has a poor reputation as a corporate citizen. (Pollution, poor service, etc.)
Presently
0 1 2 3 4 5 6 7 8 9
+-+-+-+-+-+-+-+-+-+
0 1 2 3 4 5 6 7 8 9
Ideally
The organization is highly regarded as a corporate citizen.

2.06	The organization's image is not a major concern of management.	Presently 0 1 2 3 4 5 6 7 8 9 +-+-+-+-+-+-+-+-+-+ 0 1 2 3 4 5 6 7 8 9 Ideally.	The organization's image is a priority concern of management.
2.07	The organization is perceived as being out-dated in its technology.	Presently 0 1 2 3 4 5 6 7 8 9 +-+-+-+-+-+-+-+-+-+ 0 1 2 3 4 5 6 7 8 9 Ideally	The organization is seen as a leader in its field, using advanced technology.

Value-Analysis Profile 3

Management Philosophy and Culture

3.01 The organization has no statement of management philosophy and values.

Presently
0 1 2 3 4 5 6 7 8 9
+-+-+-+-+-+-+-+-+-+-+
0 1 2 3 4 5 6 7 8 9
Ideally

The organization has a published statement of its philosophy and values.

3.02 There is no consistent basis of philosophy for the development of company policies.

Presently
0 1 2 3 4 5 6 7 8 9
+-+-+-+-+-+-+-+-+-+-+
0 1 2 3 4 5 6 7 8 9
Ideally

The organization's philosophy is used as a consistent basis for policy formulation.

3.03 The individual is viewed primarily as an object of production and profit.

Presently
0 1 2 3 4 5 6 7 8 9
+-+-+-+-+-+-+-+-+-+-+
0 1 2 3 4 5 6 7 8 9
Ideally

The individual is valued as a key resource of the company, with a personal contribution to make.

3.04 Management feels that people require external motivation and control with strong supervision.

Presently
0 1 2 3 4 5 6 7 8 9
+-+-+-+-+-+-+-+-+-+-+
0 1 2 3 4 5 6 7 8 9
Ideally

Management feels that people can be internally motivated and can exercise self-control on the job.

3.05 In management's view a person's importance is based upon his job and role in the organization.

Presently
0 1 2 3 4 5 6 7 8 9
+-+-+-+-+-+-+-+-+-+-+
0 1 2 3 4 5 6 7 8 9
Ideally

In management's view every person is considered important regardless of job level.

Appendices 173

3.06 A high personnel turnover rate is accepted as normal by management.
Presently
0 1 2 3 4 5 6 7 8 9
+-+-+-+-+-+-+-+-+-+
0 1 2 3 4 5 6 7 8 9
Ideally.
Long-term employment and job security are company policy.

3.07 Management perceives its power and authority to come from position.
Presently
0 1 2 3 4 5 6 7 8 9
+-+-+-+-+-+-+-+-+-+
0 1 2 3 4 5 6 7 8 9
Ideally
Management perceives its power and authority to be based on leadership skills, knowledge, and trust.

3.08 Racial and sexual discrimination is condoned in the organization.
Presently
0 1 2 3 4 5 6 7 8 9
+-+-+-+-+-+-+-+-+-+
0 1 2 3 4 5 6 7 8 9
Ideally
Racial and sexual discrimination are unacceptable.

3.09 It is assumed that labour and management are in an adversarial relationship.
Presently
0 1 2 3 4 5 6 7 8 9
+-+-+-+-+-+-+-+-+-+
0 1 2 3 4 5 6 7 8 9
Ideally
Labour-management relations are based on co-operation.

3.10 Individual self-interest is the primary motivator in this organization.
Presently
0 1 2 3 4 5 6 7 8 9
+-+-+-+-+-+-+-+-+-+
0 1 2 3 4 5 6 7 8 9
Ideally
Individual self-interest is balanced by a concern for the good of the organization.

3.11 Individual competition is the accepted mode of operation in the organization.
Presently
0 1 2 3 4 5 6 7 8 9
+-+-+-+-+-+-+-+-+-+
0 1 2 3 4 5 6 7 8 9
Ideally
Co-operation and teamwork is the norm in the organization.

174 The Faith-Work Connection

3.12 Individual respect is based upon position in the organization.

Presently
0 1 2 3 4 5 6 7 8 9
+-+-+-+-+-+-+-+-+-+
0 1 2 3 4 5 6 7 8 9
Ideally.

Individual respect is based on job performance and service to the organization.

3.13 The organization is simply a place to work, with little sense of pride or loyalty among the employees.

Presently
0 1 2 3 4 5 6 7 8 9
+-+-+-+-+-+-+-+-+-+
0 1 2 3 4 5 6 7 8 9
Ideally

The organization is seen as a community, with a feeling of pride and loyalty among employees.

3.14 An authoritarian leadership style is regarded as a sign of strength.

Presently
0 1 2 3 4 5 6 7 8 9
+-+-+-+-+-+-+-+-+-+
0 1 2 3 4 5 6 7 8 9
Ideally

A democratic and supportive leadership is regarded as the most effective style.

3.15 Corporate success is seen solely in terms of economic growth and the bottom line.

Presently
0 1 2 3 4 5 6 7 8 9
+-+-+-+-+-+-+-+-+-+
0 1 2 3 4 5 6 7 8 9
Ideally

Corporate success is seen in terms of the company spirit and the ability to provide quality products and service.

3.16 Management is only responsible for achieving the most efficient operation with the highest return on investment.

Presently
0 1 2 3 4 5 6 7 8 9
+-+-+-+-+-+-+-+-+-+
0 1 2 3 4 5 6 7 8 9
Ideally

Management is responsible for achieving an efficient operation as well as being concerned with preserving the environment.

3.17 In this organization justice is perceived primarily as the protection of property rights.

Presently
0 1 2 3 4 5 6 7 8 9
+-+-+-+-+-+-+-+-+-+
0 1 2 3 4 5 6 7 8 9
Ideally

In this organization justice is understood as the protection of human rights as well as property rights.

3.18 Business has no responsibility beyond the efficient generation of maximum profits.

Presently
0 1 2 3 4 5 6 7 8 9
+-+-+-+-+-+-+-+-+-+
0 1 2 3 4 5 6 7 8 9
Ideally

Business has a responsibility as a corporate citizen for the preservation of its country's culture as well as generating profits.

Value-Analysis Profile 4

Experiencing a Sense of Community in the Workplace

4.01 The development of a feeling of community within the workforce is not a management priority.

Presently
0 1 2 3 4 5 6 7 8 9
+-+-+-+-+-+-+-+-+-+-+
0 1 2 3 4 5 6 7 8 9
Ideally

The development of a feeling of community within the workplace is a priority.

4.02 Individual competition is the driving force within our organization.

Presently
0 1 2 3 4 5 6 7 8 9
+-+-+-+-+-+-+-+-+-+-+
0 1 2 3 4 5 6 7 8 9
Ideally

Working together in trusting relationships is the way we function in our organization.

4.03 Short-term employment and lack of job security are the norm in our organization.

Presently
0 1 2 3 4 5 6 7 8 9
+-+-+-+-+-+-+-+-+-+-+
0 1 2 3 4 5 6 7 8 9
Ideally

Long-term employment and job security are the norm in our organization.

4.04 Management believes in "the survival of the fittest."

Presently
0 1 2 3 4 5 6 7 8 9
+-+-+-+-+-+-+-+-+-+-+
0 1 2 3 4 5 6 7 8 9
Ideally

Management expresses care and concern for all employees.

4.05 A hierarchy of social distinction is built into the different levels of management.

Presently
0 1 2 3 4 5 6 7 8 9
+-+-+-+-+-+-+-+-+-+-+
0 1 2 3 4 5 6 7 8 9
Ideally

Social distinctions between different levels of management are minimized.

Appendices 177

4.06 Property rights are given highest priority in this organization.

Presently
0 1 2 3 4 5 6 7 8 9
+-+-+-+-+-+-+-+-+-+
0 1 2 3 4 5 6 7 8 9
Ideally

Human rights are more important than property rights in this organization.

4.07 Individual fulfilment and self respect are based upon position in the organization.

Presently
0 1 2 3 4 5 6 7 8 9
+-+-+-+-+-+-+-+-+-+
0 1 2 3 4 5 6 7 8 9
Ideally

Individual fulfilment and self-respect are based on one's contribution to the corporate community.

4.08 The primary emphasis of our organization is on the task and profit.

Presently
0 1 2 3 4 5 6 7 8 9
+-+-+-+-+-+-+-+-+-+
0 1 2 3 4 5 6 7 8 9
Ideally

Our organization maintains a balanced emphasis on the needs of the employees as well as task and profit.

4.09 Personal power and position is the major basis for human relationships and making decisions.

Presently
0 1 2 3 4 5 6 7 8 9
+-+-+-+-+-+-+-+-+-+
0 1 2 3 4 5 6 7 8 9
Ideally

Consensus through consultation is the preferred basis for governing human relationships and making decisions.

4.10 Employees are encouraged to work independantly of one another in this organization.

Presently
0 1 2 3 4 5 6 7 8 9
+-+-+-+-+-+-+-+-+-+
0 1 2 3 4 5 6 7 8 9
Ideally

Employees are encouraged to work in team relationships.

Value-Analysis Profile 5

Management Leadership Style in Your Company

5.01 Management is unpredictable and does not inspire confidence and trust in employees.
    Presently 0 1 2 3 4 5 6 7 8 9
    +-+-+-+-+-+-+-+-+-+
    0 1 2 3 4 5 6 7 8 9 Ideally
    Management is consistent and is trusted by everyone.

5.02 Management discloses only the information it thinks employees should have to do their jobs.
    Presently 0 1 2 3 4 5 6 7 8 9
    +-+-+-+-+-+-+-+-+-+
    0 1 2 3 4 5 6 7 8 9 Ideally
    Management openly shares all information with employees.

5.03 When faced with a problem, managers rely heavily on what has been done in the past.
    Presently 0 1 2 3 4 5 6 7 8 9
    +-+-+-+-+-+-+-+-+-+
    0 1 2 3 4 5 6 7 8 9 Ideally
    When faced with a problem, managers are skilled in diagnosing the problem and finding creative solutions.

5.04 As professionals, managers feel they should only display their strengths.
    Presently 0 1 2 3 4 5 6 7 8 9
    +-+-+-+-+-+-+-+-+-+
    0 1 2 3 4 5 6 7 8 9 Ideally
    As professionals, managers are unafraid of acknowledging their weaknesses.

5.05 Managers cannot allow themselves to the luxury of time to consider the psychological needs of their staff.

Presently
0 1 2 3 4 5 6 7 8 9
+-+-+-+-+-+-+-+-+-+
0 1 2 3 4 5 6 7 8 9
Ideally

Managers feel that they must find time to consider the whole employee.

5.06 Managers do not want to create waves and react to events as best they can.

Presently
0 1 2 3 4 5 6 7 8 9
+-+-+-+-+-+-+-+-+-+
0 1 2 3 4 5 6 7 8 9
Ideally.

Managers take initiatives and assume responsibility for risks they take.

5.07 Managers consider their staff as mature adults and professionals who do not require feedback or non-material recognition.

Presently
0 1 2 3 4 5 6 7 8 9
+-+-+-+-+-+-+-+-+-+
0 1 2 3 4 5 6 7 8 9
Ideally

Managers provide regular feedback and recognition to their staff on their work.

5.08 As the boss, a manager is always prepared to command and direct his employees.

Presently
0 1 2 3 4 5 6 7 8 9
+-+-+-+-+-+-+-+-+-+
0 1 2 3 4 5 6 7 8 9
Ideally

As the boss, a manager is always prepared to listen and look for opportunities to serve his employees.

5.09 Managers are realistic and concern themselves primarily with the day-to-day operation.

Presently
0 1 2 3 4 5 6 7 8 9
+-+-+-+-+-+-+-+-+-+
0 1 2 3 4 5 6 7 8 9
Ideally

Managers anticipate change and have a future orientation and a vision.

180 The Faith-Work Connection

5.10 Managers tend to think that people are basically lazy and must be coerced to work hard.

Presently
0 1 2 3 4 5 6 7 8 9
+-+-+-+-+-+-+-+-+-+
0 1 2 3 4 5 6 7 8 9
Ideally

Managers believe that people are basically self-motivating and under the right conditions will choose to work hard.

5.11 Managers tend to believe in tight control and supervision.

Presently
0 1 2 3 4 5 6 7 8 9
+-+-+-+-+-+-+-+-+-+
0 1 2 3 4 5 6 7 8 9
Ideally

Managers tend to believe in trust and minimum supervision.

5.12 Managers tend to have an authoritarian style.

Presently
0 1 2 3 4 5 6 7 8 9
+-+-+-+-+-+-+-+-+-+
0 1 2 3 4 5 6 7 8 9
Ideally

Managers tend to be supportive and use an enabling style.

5.13 Managers tend to keep their own counsel and make unilateral decisions.

Presently
0 1 2 3 4 5 6 7 8 9
+-+-+-+-+-+-+-+-+-+
0 1 2 3 4 5 6 7 8 9
Ideally

Managers tend to share decision making on a team basis.

5.14 Managers give priority to production and profit.

Presently
0 1 2 3 4 5 6 7 8 9
+-+-+-+-+-+-+-+-+-+
0 1 2 3 4 5 6 7 8 9
Ideally

Managers give priority to developing the full potential of the workforce.

5.15 Managers tend to believe in individual competitiveness as the basis for management excellence.

Presently
0 1 2 3 4 5 6 7 8 9
+-+-+-+-+-+-+-+-+-+
0 1 2 3 4 5 6 7 8 9
Ideally

Managers tend to believe in a co-operative team spirit as a basis for management excellence.

Value-Analysis Profile 6

Organizational Structure

6.01 The company organizational structure is an heirarchical pyramid.

Presently
0 1 2 3 4 5 6 7 8 9
+-+-+-+-+-+-+-+-+-+
0 1 2 3 4 5 6 7 8 9
Ideally

The company organizational structure is relatively flat, with the number of authority levels kept to a minimum.

6.02 Most decisions are made by senior management and passed down the organizational line to those who produce the goods and services.

Presently
0 1 2 3 4 5 6 7 8 9
+-+-+-+-+-+-+-+-+-+
0 1 2 3 4 5 6 7 8 9
Ideally

Decisions are made as close to the action as possible.

6.03 The company organization includes a large middle-management component and extended lines of communication.

Presently
0 1 2 3 4 5 6 7 8 9
+-+-+-+-+-+-+-+-+-+
0 1 2 3 4 5 6 7 8 9
Ideally

The company organization keeps the middle management component to a minimum and maintains short lines of communication.

182 The Faith-Work Connection

6.04 The organizational structure is based upon highly specialized units.

 Presently
 0 1 2 3 4 5 6 7 8 9
 +-+-+-+-+-+-+-+-+-+
 0 1 2 3 4 5 6 7 8 9
 Ideally

Units involving many functions are built into the organization.

6.05 Extended and unclear lines of authority make it difficult to achieve end-product accountability.

 Presently
 0 1 2 3 4 5 6 7 8 9
 +-+-+-+-+-+-+-+-+-+
 0 1 2 3 4 5 6 7 8 9
 Ideally

Product cost centres are clearly defined within the organization, ensuring end-product accountability.

6.06 Organizational structure provides for a strong central control of production units.

 Presently
 0 1 2 3 4 5 6 7 8 9
 +-+-+-+-+-+-+-+-+-+
 0 1 2 3 4 5 6 7 8 9
 Ideally.

Control and monitoring are the responsibility of production units.

6.07 The organizational structure provides for a large central corporate planning function.

 Presently
 0 1 2 3 4 5 6 7 8 9
 +-+-+-+-+-+-+-+-+-+
 0 1 2 3 4 5 6 7 8 9
 Ideally

The planning function is provided by individual units within broadly defined corporate guidelines provided by a small central group.

Value-Analysis Profile 7

Human Resourcing

6.01 My boss spends next to no time on career planning and development for his staff.

　　　Presently
　　0 1 2 3 4 5 6 7 8 9
　　+-+-+-+-+-+-+-+-+-+
　　0 1 2 3 4 5 6 7 8 9
　　　　Ideally

My boss considers the careers of his staff important and spends an appreciable amount of time on planning for their career development.

7.02 Much money is spent on sending staff on courses which are not considered either relevant to their jobs or their future development.

　　　Presently
　　0 1 2 3 4 5 6 7 8 9
　　+-+-+-+-+-+-+-+-+-+
　　0 1 2 3 4 5 6 7 8 9
　　　　Ideally

Employees are sent on courses with direct bearing to their jobs and their longer-term career goals.

7.03 Executive promotions are based on personal relationships rather than on competence and performance.

　　　Presently
　　0 1 2 3 4 5 6 7 8 9
　　+-+-+-+-+-+-+-+-+-+
　　0 1 2 3 4 5 6 7 8 9
　　　　Ideally

Executive promotions are earned and are based on merit and achievement.

7.04 Even though promotion opportunities are advertised openly, selection often appears to be predetermined.

　　　Presently
　　0 1 2 3 4 5 6 7 8 9
　　+-+-+-+-+-+-+-+-+-+
　　0 1 2 3 4 5 6 7 8 9
　　　　Ideally

Promotions are advertised openly and the most qualified person usually gets the job.

184   The Faith-Work Connection

7.05	Promotions primarily occur from within the same department or organizational unit, and specialization in one functional area is favoured.	Presently 0 1 2 3 4 5 6 7 8 9 +-+-+-+-+-+-+-+-+-+ 0 1 2 3 4 5 6 7 8 9 Ideally	Cross organizational appointments are encouraged and carried out on a regular basis as a means of enhancing staff development and broadening employees' knowledge of the organization.
7.06	Racial and sexual discrimination are condoned.	Presently 0 1 2 3 4 5 6 7 8 9 +-+-+-+-+-+-+-+-+-+ 0 1 2 3 4 5 6 7 8 9 Ideally.	All human discrimination is unacceptable.
7.07	Economic rewards form the primary basis for work motivation.	Presently 0 1 2 3 4 5 6 7 8 9 +-+-+-+-+-+-+-+-+-+ 0 1 2 3 4 5 6 7 8 9 Ideally	Motivation is derived through meaningful work as well as economic rewards.
7.08	Competition between individuals is encouraged without regard to the benefit of the whole organization.	Presently 0 1 2 3 4 5 6 7 8 9 +-+-+-+-+-+-+-+-+-+ 0 1 2 3 4 5 6 7 8 9 Ideally	Co-operation and commitment to the organizational community is encouraged, emphasizing the well-being of the whole organization.
7.09	Executive assessment is conducted informally, and not based upon a structured career-development program.	Presently 0 1 2 3 4 5 6 7 8 9 +-+-+-+-+-+-+-+-+-+ 0 1 2 3 4 5 6 7 8 9 Ideally	Executive assessment is formally conducted, and is based upon a well-managed career development.

Value-Analysis Profile 8

Labour-Management Relations

8.01 Labour is considered as a commodity to be bought and sold.
   Presently
   0 1 2 3 4 5 6 7 8 9
   +-+-+-+-+-+-+-+-+-+
   0 1 2 3 4 5 6 7 8 9
   Ideally
   Labour is a valuable part of of the organization and considered an important resource.

8.02 Safe working conditions are provided only within legal requirements.
   Presently
   0 1 2 3 4 5 6 7 8 9
   +-+-+-+-+-+-+-+-+-+
   0 1 2 3 4 5 6 7 8 9
   Ideally
   Safe and healthy working conditions are provided which exceed legal requirements.

8.03 Labour has little job security.
   Presently
   0 1 2 3 4 5 6 7 8 9
   +-+-+-+-+-+-+-+-+-+
   0 1 2 3 4 5 6 7 8 9
   Ideally
   Long-term job security is provided.

8.04 Company policies encourage workers to be passive and dependent in their work situation.
   Presently
   0 1 2 3 4 5 6 7 8 9
   +-+-+-+-+-+-+-+-+-+
   0 1 2 3 4 5 6 7 8 9
   Ideally
   Company policies encourage workers to participate in decisions and to take initiatives on the job.

8.05	Workers are not expected to make a creative contribution to the work process, and few suggestions for improvement are made by employees.	Presently 0 1 2 3 4 5 6 7 8 9 +-+-+-+-+-+-+-+-+-+ 0 1 2 3 4 5 6 7 8 9 Ideally	Workers are expected to make a creative contribution. Improvement suggestions are numerous and well rewarded.
8.06	Our organization experiences a high rate of absenteeism.	Presently 0 1 2 3 4 5 6 7 8 9 +-+-+-+-+-+-+-+-+-+ 0 1 2 3 4 5 6 7 8 9 Ideally.	Our organization experiences a low rate of absenteeism.
8.07	Our organization experiences a large number of employee grievances.	Presently 0 1 2 3 4 5 6 7 8 9 +-+-+-+-+-+-+-+-+-+ 0 1 2 3 4 5 6 7 8 9 Ideally	Our organization experiences few employee grievances.
8.08	Middle management directs and controls the work process and provides the quality control.	Presently 0 1 2 3 4 5 6 7 8 9 +-+-+-+-+-+-+-+-+-+ 0 1 2 3 4 5 6 7 8 9 Ideally	Middle management shares decision making with workers who maintain their own standards.
8.09	Labour and management begin contract negotiations by offering or demanding unrealistic extremes and use mutual intimidation to try to arrive at a compromise agreement.	Presently 0 1 2 3 4 5 6 7 8 9 +-+-+-+-+-+-+-+-+-+ 0 1 2 3 4 5 6 7 8 9 Ideally	Labour and management negotiators state their essential conditions for an acceptable solution and then function as a single problem-solving team to reach a mutual agreement.

		Presently	
8.10	Labour-management negotiators usually adopt an adversarial position.	0 1 2 3 4 5 6 7 8 9 +-+-+-+-+-+-+-+-+-+ 0 1 2 3 4 5 6 7 8 9 Ideally	Labour-management representatives can approach contract negotiations as co-operative problem solvers.
8.11	The goal in contract negotiations is victory.	0 1 2 3 4 5 6 7 8 9 +-+-+-+-+-+-+-+-+-+ 0 1 2 3 4 5 6 7 8 9 Ideally	The goal in contract negotiations is to efficiently and amicably reach a wise agreement that suits both parties.
8.12	Distrust and guarded communication is the underlying principle in the relationship between the labour-management negotiators.	0 1 2 3 4 5 6 7 8 9 +-+-+-+-+-+-+-+-+-+ 0 1 2 3 4 5 6 7 8 9 Ideally	Trust and open communication are the bases of the relationship between the labour-management negotiators.
8.13	Both sides try to hold firmly to their fixed positions.	0 1 2 3 4 5 6 7 8 9 +-+-+-+-+-+-+-+-+-+ 0 1 2 3 4 5 6 7 8 9 Ideally	The negotiations focus on mutual benefits rather than on fixed positions.
8.14	Labour and management focus on short-term financial gain.	0 1 2 3 4 5 6 7 8 9 +-+-+-+-+-+-+-+-+-+ 0 1 2 3 4 5 6 7 8 9 Ideally	Labour and management focus on long-term goals which are in the interest of both parties.

Value-Analysis Profile 9

Technological Development and Utilization

9.01 Work is organized so that people function as extensions of the machines.

Presently
0 1 2 3 4 5 6 7 8 9
+-+-+-+-+-+-+-+-+-+
0 1 2 3 4 5 6 7 8 9
Ideally

Work is organized so that human needs and values determine the way in which technology and machines are used.

9.02 Human-resource management is subservient to technical development, scientific specialization, and financial performance.

Presently
0 1 2 3 4 5 6 7 8 9
+-+-+-+-+-+-+-+-+-+
0 1 2 3 4 5 6 7 8 9
Ideally

Human-resource management is balanced with technical and financial performance management for overall effectiveness.

9.03 Technical design is developed without concern for human factors.

Presently
0 1 2 3 4 5 6 7 8 9
+-+-+-+-+-+-+-+-+-+
0 1 2 3 4 5 6 7 8 9
Ideally

Job design balances people needs with technological needs.

9.04 Wherever possible technological developments are used to eliminate jobs.

Presently
0 1 2 3 4 5 6 7 8 9
+-+-+-+-+-+-+-+-+-+
0 1 2 3 4 5 6 7 8 9
Ideally

The organization takes responsibility for the redeployment of people displaced by technology.

9.05	Management makes unilateral decisions regarding the introduction of technology.	Presently 0 1 2 3 4 5 6 7 8 9 +-+-+-+-+-+-+-+-+-+ 0 1 2 3 4 5 6 7 8 9 Ideally	Management consults with those whose work will be be affected, before introducing new technology.
9.06	When jobs are eliminated, people are terminated.	Presently 0 1 2 3 4 5 6 7 8 9 +-+-+-+-+-+-+-+-+-+ 0 1 2 3 4 5 6 7 8 9 Ideally.	When jobs are eliminated, people are retrained for different work.
9.07	Technological change tends to be resisted by management.	Presently 0 1 2 3 4 5 6 7 8 9 +-+-+-+-+-+-+-+-+-+ 0 1 2 3 4 5 6 7 8 9 Ideally	Management recognizes that technological change is essential for survival and growth.
9.08	Labour unions tend to resist the introduction of new technology as a threat to jobs.	Presently 0 1 2 3 4 5 6 7 8 9 +-+-+-+-+-+-+-+-+-+ 0 1 2 3 4 5 6 7 8 9 Ideally	The introduction of new technology is worked out in consultation with the union to ensure a just arrangement regarding jobs.
9.09	The company spends a minimum on research and development and relies on past and present product success.	Presently 0 1 2 3 4 5 6 7 8 9 +-+-+-+-+-+-+-+-+-+ 0 1 2 3 4 5 6 7 8 9 Ideally	The company invests heavily in research and development in order to maintain a competitive advantage.

Value-Analysis Profile 10

The Operational System

10.01 Production is monitored and controlled by a nonproduction group.

Presently
0 1 2 3 4 5 6 7 8 9
+-+-+-+-+-+-+-+-+-+
0 1 2 3 4 5 6 7 8 9
Ideally

Production costs and quality are controlled by the production group through quality circles, etc.

10.02 Work is highly specialized and structured, limiting initiatives and creativity.

Presently
0 1 2 3 4 5 6 7 8 9
+-+-+-+-+-+-+-+-+-+
0 1 2 3 4 5 6 7 8 9
Ideally

Initiative and creativity are encouraged by giving individuals a broader scope of work.

10.03 Individual performance is valued more highly than team performance.

Presently
0 1 2 3 4 5 6 7 8 9
+-+-+-+-+-+-+-+-+-+
0 1 2 3 4 5 6 7 8 9
Ideally

Team performance is encouraged and rewarded.

10.04 The reward system and determination of promotions appears unclear in the minds of employees.

Presently
0 1 2 3 4 5 6 7 8 9
+-+-+-+-+-+-+-+-+-+
0 1 2 3 4 5 6 7 8 9
Ideally

The reward system and determination of promotions are clearly understood by everyone.

10.05 Communication between supervisors and employees is restricted to correcting job performance.

Presently
0 1 2 3 4 5 6 7 8 9
+-+-+-+-+-+-+-+-+-+
0 1 2 3 4 5 6 7 8 9
Ideally

Work performance feedback is frequent and emphasizes positive affirmation.

10.06 Planning and decisions are made at the top and communicated down the line.

Presently
0 1 2 3 4 5 6 7 8 9
+-+-+-+-+-+-+-+-+-+
0 1 2 3 4 5 6 7 8 9
Ideally

Open communication encourages participation in planning and decision making at all levels.

10.07 The organization's goal statements are seldom referred to and are not taken too seriously.

Presently
0 1 2 3 4 5 6 7 8 9
+-+-+-+-+-+-+-+-+-+
0 1 2 3 4 5 6 7 8 9
Ideally

The organization's goal statements are taken seriously, they are understood and accepted by everyone, and provide the basis for all decision making.

10.08 Performance standards for work are arbitrarily used and are not clearly understood by all employees.

Presently
0 1 2 3 4 5 6 7 8 9
+-+-+-+-+-+-+-+-+-+
0 1 2 3 4 5 6 7 8 9
Ideally

Performance standards were developed jointly by management and employees: they are clear and understood by everyone.

10.09 Many employees are under-employed and poorly utilized.

Presently
0 1 2 3 4 5 6 7 8 9
+-+-+-+-+-+-+-+-+-+
Ideally

Effort is made by management to establish an optimum job-person fit.

10.10 When work levels are low, employees are laid off.

Presently
0 1 2 3 4 5 6 7 8 9
+-+-+-+-+-+-+-+-+-+
0 1 2 3 4 5 6 7 8 9
Ideally

When work levels are low employees are retained and used in other ways.

10.11 Employees are considered as dispenssable commodities.

Presently
0 1 2 3 4 5 6 7 8 9
+-+-+-+-+-+-+-+-+-+
0 1 2 3 4 5 6 7 8 9
Ideally

Employees are considered as valuable resources

10.12 Adversarial and competitive relationships between workers are the norm.

Presently
0 1 2 3 4 5 6 7 8 9
+-+-+-+-+-+-+-+-+-+
0 1 2 3 4 5 6 7 8 9
Ideally

Co-operative relationships between workers are expected.

10.13 Employee rewards are predominantly wage and security oriented.

Presently
0 1 2 3 4 5 6 7 8 9
+-+-+-+-+-+-+-+-+-+
0 1 2 3 4 5 6 7 8 9
Ideally

Employee rewards meet self-esteem and social as well as economic needs.

10.14 Suggestions for improvements are not encouraged, and there is no effective procedure.

Presently
0 1 2 3 4 5 6 7 8 9
+-+-+-+-+-+-+-+-+-+
0 1 2 3 4 5 6 7 8 9
Ideally

Suggestions for improvements are encouraged, and an effective procedure is used.

10.15 Suggestions for improvements that are made are not usually acknowledged or accepted.

Presently
0 1 2 3 4 5 6 7 8 9
+-+-+-+-+-+-+-+-+-+
0 1 2 3 4 5 6 7 8 9
Ideally

All suggestions are acknowledged and a high percent are accepted and implemented.

10.16 Individuals achieving difficult corporate objectives and setting high performance standards are not publically recognized.

       Presently
0 1 2 3 4 5 6 7 8 9
+-+-+-+-+-+-+-+-+-+
0 1 2 3 4 5 6 7 8 9
        Ideally

High achievers are given public recognition.

(Copyright 1983, Management Support Systems)

Appendix 6
Office Morale and Strife

Case Study 1

You are twenty-seven years old, and having just moved to this town, have accepted a position as a policy clerk with the local branch of Polka-Dot Insurance Company.

You were interviewed by the branch manager, and were delighted to be offered the job; you liked the manager's style, the job sounded interesting, with an opportunity to learn and progress, and the pay was good.

Now it's mid-day of your first day at the new job, and you're wondering whether you've made a terrible mistake.

— the manager is out (apparently he often is) and there seems to be no supervision or system.
— morale among the other eight employees seems very low; there is a lot of criticism of the company, and of the manager.
— in particular the clerk at the next desk seems set on making your life miserable, and is a chronic complainer.

For discussion
— How can you, as a concerned Christian, start to improve this office situation?
— How are you to deal with the clerk at the next desk?
— Should you take your concerns to the manager who hired you? What would be your expectations from doing that?
— What do Matt. 5:13-16 and Matt. 5:43-48 say to this situation?

Appendix 7
Overtime and Personal Priorities

Case Study 2

The Tiger Supply and Service Co. Ltd. is a Canada-wide organization, warehousing and wholesaling a wide range of consumer products. The Winnipeg office includes the accounting and computer departments for the whole of Canada.

Jane Gray is the senior computer programmer — reporting to the manager of computer systems, Mike McFarlane — and has worked there for three years. She is attractive, technically very competent, but quiet and somewhat shy. She is thirty-two, married, with two young children.

McFarlane is forty-five, single, very proficient and diligent at his work (and knows it). He drives himself hard, working long hours and often over weekends.

Last Thursday in mid-afternoon, McFarlane asked Jane Gray to work on into the evening with him as there was a problem with a new system coming on-line. Jane had plans that evening for an outing with her husband and children.

This was the third time in a month that Jane was asked to work overtime (being salaried, she is not paid for overtime worked).

For Discussion
— Role play a meeting between Jane, Mike, and Mike's boss as they discuss Jane's reluctance to work overtime.
— Deal with Mike's tendency to be a "workaholic."
— Jane's inflexibility about working overtime.
— As a group, relate this scene to Luke 12:13-34.

Appendix 8
A Bad Work Environment — Stay or Quit?

Case Study 3

I would like to tell you about my friend Charlie. He is what you would call a "blue-collar worker." He works in the rolling mill of one of Canada's largest steel companies. Charlie's a good man: church-goer all his life, family man, a really pleasant, gentle man, who somehow seems out of tune with the harshness of his work environment.

Charlie was telling me the other day that he is thinking of quitting his job. "When I started there eleven years ago, I knew it would be a tough scene, but I was confident that my faith was strong and that perhaps I could spread a little of it. Now, I realize I was a dreamer. That's a pagan world in there — the obscenities and blasphemies all day long are really getting to me. Now I have a new foreman, and he is the worst of the lot."

My friend faces a decision that many of us are up against: how long do I dig in my heels and strive to be an agent for change, and at what stage do I quit?

For Discussion
— If you were Charlie, what factors would you consider before deciding to stay or quit?
— What strategies for change are open to you?
— Compare Matt. 10:14 and Eph. 6:10-11.

Appendix 9
Labour-Management Conflict

Case Study 4

Tom McDonald is a middle manager for Certified Automotive Systems Limited, a company that makes parts under contract with two of the big auto manufacturers. In the plant where Tom works, there are 700 employees, 500 of whom are members of a union and 200 are not. Tom is manager of quality control; his job is to ensure that the products they make are to a satisfactory standard.

Tom's boss, plant manager Bill Dunsford, is a stickler for perfection and very inflexible and intolerant of error. He wants 100 per cent production and no rejects.

One of the shop stewards, Art Small, seems to Tom to be ignoring the need for the company to survive in a very competitive field. He is constantly initiating grievance procedures claiming violation of the union agreement. He often challenges Tom's policies and actions as being anti-labour. Tom and Art have just come out of a stormy meeting at which Art has threatened to bring the men out on strike unless Tom withdraws a memorandum he issued dealing with a 20 per cent rejection of last week's production.

"If we go on like this, we'll be out of business," says Tom.

"If you'd only consult us before setting production quotas, you wouldn't be asking us to do the impossible," responds Art.

For Discussion
— What Christian values should Tom use to deal with this situation?
— What steps can Tom and Art take to ease the polarisation between management and labour?
— How can Tom deal with his personal feelings of rejection and isolation?

Appendix 10
Technology Versus People

Case Study 5

When the provincial government tries to be efficient, most of us are ready to sit up and take notice. But let me tell you what happened recently where I work.

My name is Cynthia, and I'm a secretary in one of the big government departments and enjoy working for and with three very pleasant and efficient bosses. I really thought I had it made for some years to come.

Now along comes an efficiency expert who has told our office manager that we are to convert to word-processing equipment that will enable each of us to do the typing for five bosses instead of three, and will eliminate unnecessary interruptions. We secretaries read three messages in that: we will work harder, there will be fewer of us, and we will sit at machines all day. What about the stories we read about eye-strain and radiation hazards? I tell you, I'm just about ready to quit!

Our office manager is really quite weak; why doesn't he just dig his heels in, and say that it's a poor move? Or is it? I'm so confused!

For Discussion
— Role play a department meeting between bosses, secretaries, and office manager, called to resolve the unrest and protest of the secretaries.
— What Christian values are relevant to Cynthia's position?
— How is an enterprise like a modern office to maintain and affirm the worth and dignity of employees?
— Discuss this scenario in the light of Psalm 8.

Appendix 11
Over the Hump

Case Study 6

The top management of a business firm in a highly competitive area has made the decision to reduce costs and manpower in order to remain competitive, to provide a fair return to shareholders on investment, and to continue to pay the salaries and related benefits that are superior to their major comptitors.

A specific situation as a result of this decision has now emerged. Jack, a loyal employee (age fifty-four) with twenty-one years in the company has now reached the limit of his abilities. Since there is a continuous upgrading of standards in his professional area and increasing responsibilities within the company at his level, this man will soon be unable to provide satisfactory performance. There is no other suitable job, and the retirement plans are generous and will take care of all his reasonable financial needs. If this employee is not laid off, then Bill, a recently hired young man with an advanced degree in the same professional area, must be asked to resign. Yet his supervisor feels that he has high potential, that he is ready for rapid promotion within the company, and that his professional qualifications are superior to those of people with a similar professional background and position in competitive companies.

Personal Questions

1. What kind of assumptions or ground rules would a concerned Christian likely bring to this situation?

200 The Faith-Work Connection

2 Which of your own values (things you really care about) are involved in this situation?

_____
_____
_____

Group Questions

You are responsible for making the choice between Jack and Bill.

1 What drives are motivating people in this situation?
2 What pressures are affecting this situation?
3 Would you keep Jack and let Bill go?
4 Would you keep Bill and let Jack go?

Note: This case is based on Malcolm W. Eckel, *Case Studies from the Ethics of Decision Making* (New York: Morehouse-Barlow Co., 1968).

Appendix 12
Scanning Your Work Environment

What are some of the ways you can minister to the spirit of your organization? What needs to be changed from a Christian value perspective?

Reflect on the atmosphere of your office or workplace.
(Circle the numbers that refect your situation.)

1 Fear and animosity	1 2 3 4 5 6 7 8 9 10	Love and caring
2 Anxiety and uncertainty	1 2 3 4 5 6 7 8 9 10	Peace and security
3 Unfairness and injustice	1 2 3 4 5 6 7 8 9 10	Fairness and justice
4 Information and ideas flow top down	1 2 3 4 5 6 7 8 9 10	Information and ideas flow in all directions
5 Distrust	1 2 3 4 5 6 7 8 9 10	Trust
6 Indifference to personal worth	1 2 3 4 5 6 7 8 9 10	People treated with dignity and respect
7 Competitive individualism	1 2 3 4 5 6 7 8 9 10	Co-operative community
8 Bosses are authoritarian	1 2 3 4 5 6 7 8 9 10	Bosses are helpful enablers
9 Alienation and disloyalty	1 2 3 4 5 6 7 8 9 10	Belonging and loyalty
10 Routine boredom	1 2 3 4 5 6 7 8 9 10	Interesting challenge
11 Personal stagnation	1 2 3 4 5 6 7 8 9 10	Opportunity for personal growth
12 Sex discrimination	1 2 3 4 5 6 7 8 9 10	Equal treatment
13 Irresponsible attitudes	1 2 3 4 5 6 7 8 9 10	Responsible attitudes

14 Dishonesty condoned	1 2 3 4 5 6 7 8 9 10	Honesty and integrity valued
15 Language profane	1 2 3 4 5 6 7 8 9 10	Language decent

What could you do to change the low ratings to higher ones?

Appendix 13
Criteria for Evaluating Public-Affairs Issues

1. *Seriousness:* How serious is the issue? How important is its resolution to the (A) company; (B) communities in which the company operates, and (C) country? What has been done about the issue by both private and public sectors?
2. *Relevance:* Will the issue affect the company? In what ways? When?
3. *Experience:* What has the company been doing in this area? How effective has this been (is there any observable impact)?
4. *Expertise:* What resources and skills does the company have which are relevant to the issue? Where are they? How available are they?
5. *Opportunity:* To what extent can the company affect the issue? Do apparent business opportunities exist for addressing the issue?
6. *Costs:* What are the estimated costs of not addressing the issue for the (A) company, (B) communities, and (C) country?

(Human Resources Network)

Appendix 14
A Basis for a Social Audit

The Process and Substantive Areas

Areas for Evaluation	Specific Questions for Analysis
1 The role of the board of directors: Corporate public policy formulation	1.1 What is the board of directors' public role? 1.2 What are the emerging issues of governance? 1.3 Is the board organizing to define and direct public policy?
2 Managing public strategies	2.1 How does management define and institutionalize public strategies? 2.2 Social forecasting as a management tool 2.3 Social accounting as a management tool 2.4 Evaluation and monitoring of social performance 2.5 Analysis and key management briefing on relevant public issues
3 Corporate philanthropy and volunteerism	3.1 Philanthropy 3.2 Executives on loan 3.3 Employee volunteer programs

		3.4	Loans of corporate facilities for public use
4	The corporation in the community	4.1	Urban redevelopment
		4.2	Transportation
		4.3	Plan relocation
		4.4	Housing
		4.5	Law enforcement, the courts, and security
		4.6	Industry-related issues
		4.7	Public policy issues at the federal, state, and local levels
5	Health, safety and legal services	5.1	Preventive health care
		5.2	Health insurance costs
		5.3	Mental health counselling
		5.4	Health maintenance organizations
		5.5	Safety standards and regulations
		5.6	OSHA compliance systems
		5.7	Alcoholism and drug abuse programs
6	Corporations, the arts and the humanities	6.1	Architecture and design of physical facilities
		6.2	Product design
		6.3	Business art collections
		6.4	Recreation
		6.5	Cultural facilities
		6.6	Personal enrichment opportunities
7	Human resources development and employment	7.1	The corporation as an educational institution
		7.2	Job training
		7.3	Sabbaticals
		7.4	Education subsidies
		7.5	Youth

		7.6	Elderly
		7.7	The handicapped
		7.8	Prisoner and addict rehabilitation
		7.9	The hard-core unemployed
8	The environment and resources	8.1	Pollution control
		8.2	Conservation of natural resources and energy
		8.3	Land use
		8.4	Environmental impact of products
		8.5	Natural resources
9	The legal system	9.1	Judicial delay
		9.2	Regulatory reform
		9.3	Conflict resolution and avoidance
10	Consumerism	10.1	Product integrity
		10.2	Product performance
		10.3	Consumer information and education
		10.4	Marketing process
		10.5	Credit practices
		10.6	Consumer-complaint procedures
11	Women and minorities	11.1	Equal opportunity
		11.2	Job advancement
		11.3	Support for minority and women-owned businesses through purchasing
		11.4	Subcontracting
12	Corporation as a community	12.1	Job satisfaction
		12.2	Job enrichment
		12.3	Flexible scheduling
		12.4	Employee participation in management decisions

		12.5	Child care
		12.6	New forms of employee ownership of business
		12.7	The nomadic family
		12.8	Socio-economic factors of retirement
13	The developing world	13.1	Cultural impact of technological change
		13.2	Employee education and training
		13.3	Technology transfer
14	Business integrity	14.1	Business ethics
		14.2	Codes of conduct
		14.3	Public disclosure
		14.4	Political activity

(Center for Public Resources, Inc., 250 Park Avenue, New York, N.Y. 10017)

Appendix 15
My Gifts

We all have God-given gifts, "each of us has been given his special gift" (Ephesians 4:7). It is important that we identify and name our gifts so that we can develop and make the most of them. Our gifts include skills, ways of being with and relating to others individually and in groups, talents, etc.

Some of the things I do well are:_____
_____
_____

Some of my greatest achievements in life were:_____
_____
_____

Some of the things I enjoy doing most are:_____
_____
_____

Some of the things about me that others seem to notice in a complimentary way are:_____
_____
_____

Some of the things I would most like to be able to do are:_____
_____
_____

In the light of the above I think my most important gifts are:_____

Appendix 16
The Mind of Christ

"Let this mind in you which was also in Christ Jesus . . . " (Philippians 2:5) and *"Seek ye first the kingdom of God"* (Luke 12:31).

Complete the following sentences:

1   Jesus is the kind of person who_____

2   He sees the world as_____

3   He sees people as_____

4   He sees success in terms of_____

5   He regards money as_____

6   He sees human relationships in terms of_____

7   He demonstrated and calls us to follow a leadership style which is
_____
_____

8   His priorities are_____
_____
_____

9   How does Jesus regard work?_____
_____
_____

10 How does Jesus exercise or use power?_____
_____
_____

11 How does he regard property?_____
_____
_____

12 How does he regard status and authority?_____
_____
_____

13 For Jesus happiness is_____
_____
_____

How can Jesus' values and perspective be applied in our daily lives and work?
_____
_____
_____

Appendix 17
A Commissioning Service for Ministry

A hymn may be sung.

Reading: Ephesians 4:1-12

Minister: My brothers and sisters, every Christian is called to follow Jesus Christ, serving God the Father through the power of the Holy Spirit. God calls each person to a special ministry that is an appropriate expression of our own gifts and skills. Today we recognize and affirm the ministry of those who desire to make a public commitment of themselves and of their work to be used in His service. We know that God works through each and every one of us and is able to use whatever is honestly and faithfully offered.

Will those who desire to be commissioned in their ministries please stand.

When the persons are standing, the Minister says: Do you believe that you are truly called by God to serve Him through the work that is yours?

Response: I do believe that I am called.

Minister: Do you now in the presence of the church, commit yourself to express, insofar as you are able, Christian love in all of the structures, relationships, and decisions involved in that work?

Response: I do.

Minister: Will you both seek the guidance and pastoral direction of the church and also enrich the life of your congregation by sharing your experiences and insights in return?

Response: I will.

Minister: Will you look for Christ in all others, being ready to help and serve those in need in any way that your work provides?

Response: I will, with God's help.

Minister: Will you do your best to pattern your own life as well as your household, community, and profession in accordance with the teachings of Christ, striving in all things to be a wholesome example to all people?

Response: I will, with God's help.

Minister — or other leader(s): Let us pray.
(in litany form, with people saying "Amen".)

Almighty God. Look with favour upon these persons who have now reaffirmed their commitment to follow Christ and to serve in his name.
Amen.

Give them courage, patience, and vision to stand firm in the face of trials and adversity.
Amen.

Help them to discern the difficult truth and strengthen them to act upon it.
Amen

Give them the words to witness to your love in the midst of difficulties and defeats.
Amen.

Grant to them a measure of happiness that they may bring joy into situations where your people are without hope or cheer.
Amen.

Send your Holy Spirit into every place of work, every home, and every business or agency.
Amen.

Reconcile and renew every aspect of this lonely world through the work and witness of those whose ministry is spread throughout your whole creation.
Amen.

Through one another, may we come to know in all of life the healing power of your Holy Spirit and that peace which passes all understanding, through Jesus Christ our Lord.
Amen.

The service concludes with the passing of the peace and a hymn.

Appendix 18
A Responsible Christian Lifestyle

Those who follow the way of Christ are called to a life of loving responsibility. Recognizing all of life as a gift from God to be celebrated in unity with all people, and acknowledging that the resources of the earth are finite, we are called to share them as responsible stewards. Therefore, I will strive to live a simple and responsible life.

1. I will live as a citizen of the world, seeing beyond the needs of all people.
2. I will cultivate a biblical view of life, namely that the earth is the Lord's, and the purpose of life is to be found in our relationship with Christ and each other.
3. I recognize that I need the supportive fellowship of a Christian community for my personal growth and strength, in order to follow the Christian way, and to commit myself to responsible participation in a community of faith.
4. I will strive to lead a life of creative simplicity,
   — distinguishing between my real needs and greed (happiness is knowing what I can do *without*),
   — distinguishing between self-respect and pride,
   — distinguishing between necessary ownership and undue pride of possession,
   — cultivating a healthy perspective on the value of people over things.
5. I will strive to make responsible use of my time and money, sharing these resources with the needy and poor.
6. I accept myself — body, mind, and spirit, as a gift from God, and in response, I am committed to the fullest development of my whole being, physically, mentally, and spiritually.

7 I will strive to examine continually my relations with others, and to attempt to relate honestly, morally, responsibly, and lovingly to those around me.
8 I commit myself to resist any forces which tend to dehumanize people, or crush the human spirit.
9 I commit myself to join with others in reshaping institutions, in order to bring about a more just global society, in which each person has full access to the needed resources for their physical, emotional, intellectual, and spiritual growth.
10 I commit myself to occupational accountability, and in so doing I will seek to avoid the creation of products which cause harm to others.
11 I will strive to exercise conservation and avoid waste,
    — exercising restraint in the use of all forms of energy
    — using the most responsible forms of transportation
    — recycling materials whenever possible
    — resisting obsolescence by choosing the longest lasting products
    — questioning advertising, particularly when it is based on competition and status values.
12 I commit myself to personal renewal, through prayer, meditation, and study,
    — cultivating an attitude of thankfulness and hope
    — seeking the courage to take the risks involved in a life of faith.

Date _____ Signature _____

Suggested guildlines for an appropriate Christian lifestyle, based on several sources and published by the King-Bay Chaplaincy.

Notes

Introduction

1 William E. Diehl, *Christianity and Real Life* (Philadelphia: Fortress Press, 1976), p.vii.
2 G.H. Tucker, *It's Your Life, Create a Christian Lifestyle* (Toronto: Anglican Book Centre, 1977).

1 A World in Transition

1 Matt. 6:33 (KJV).
2 Harry Blamires, *The Christian Mind* (Ann Arbor: Servant Books, 1963), p. 27.
3 Thomas S. Kuhn, "The Structure of Scientific Revolutions," *International Encyclopedia of Unified Science*, I, II, 1962.
4 Lesslie Newbigin, *Honest Religion for Secular Man* (Birmingham: SCM Press, 1966), p. 32.

2 The Unshakable Kingdom

1 Address by Martin Luther King.
2 Isa. 42:1-7, 49:1-6, 50:1-9, 50:52-53, 61:1-3, 61:6-7.
3 William Stringfellow, *An Ethic for Christians and Other Aliens in a Strange Land* (Waco, Texas: Word, 1973).
4 M. Scott Peck, *The Road Less Travelled* (New York: Simon & Schuster, 1978), p. 278.
5 M. Scott Peck, *People of the Lie* (New York: Simon & Schuster, 1983), p. 42-43.
6 John 8:44 (NEB).
7 2 Cor. 11:15 (NEB).
8 Matt. 4:8-10 (NEB).
9 John 17:15 (GNB).
10 Mark 14:24, 1 Cor. 11:25 (NEB).

11 Mark 4:30-32 (NEB).
12 Luke 17:20-21 (NEB).
13 John 3:3 (NEB).
14 Mark 10:15 (NEB).
15 Luke 4:18 (NEB).
16 Luke 12:16 (NEB).
17 Robert E. Webber, *The Secular Saint* (Grand Rapids: Zondervan, 1979), p. 19.
18 Ibid., p. 25.
19 Richard H. Niebuhr, *Christ and Culture* (New York: Harper & Row, 1951), p. 43.
20 Ibid., p. 193-196.
21 Ibid., p. 228.
22 Gen. 1:28 (KJV).
23 Paul Marshall, *Thine Is the Kingdom* (Basingstoke: Marshall Morgan and Scott, 1984), p. 25.
24 James Taylor, *Two Worlds in One* (Winfield, B.C.: Woodlake Books, 1985), p. 58.
25 Ibid., p. 30.

3 The Power of Values

1 Peter Berger, "Secularity, West and East," *This World*, no. 4 (Winter, 1983), 61.
2 Russell D. Legge, "Technological and Religious Pluralism," paper presented to the Canadian Theological Society, Montreal, June 1985, part IV.
3 John F. Kavanaugh, *Following Christ in a Consumer Society* (New York: Orbis Books, 1981), p. 21.
4 G.H.Tucker, "Management Values in the Toronto Business Community." Parts 1 & 2, A Survey and Analysis, PhD. thesis, 1979.
5 Eph. 4:13 (NEB).
6 1 John 3:14 (NEB).
7 Donald H. Blocker, *Developmental Counselling* (Ronald Press).
8 Viktor Frankel, *Man's Search for Meaning* (Washington Square Press, 1963).
9 Neil Chamberlain, *The Place of Business in America's Future* (New York: Basic Books Inc., 1973).
10 T.D. Deal and A.A. Kennedy, *Corporate Cultures* (Reading: Addison-Wesley, 1982), p. 6.

11 T.S. Peters and R.H., Waterman Jr., *In Search of Excellence* (New York: Harper & Row, 1982), p. 280.

I am indebted to Oliver F. Williams and John W. Houck for their development of the relationship between values and theology in their book *Full Value*, Harper and Row, 1978.

4 Values in the Workplace

1. Russell Ackoff, "The Second Industrial Revolution," paper, The Alban Institute, Mount St. Alban, Washington, D.C., 1975, p. 6.
2. Ibid., p. 5.
3. John 1:1-3 (NEB).
4. Gen. 1:3,26 (KJV).
5. Robert K. Greenleaf, *Servant Leadership* (New York: Paulist Press, 1977), p. 141-142.
6. Richard T. Pascale and Anthony G. Athos, *The Art of Japanese Management* (New York: Simon & Schuster, 1981), p. 192.
7. Richard C. Hodgson, "Leadership that Leads," *The Business Quarterly*.
8. *Psychology Today*, December 1981, p. 81.
9. Wallace Clement, *Continental Corporate Power* (Toronto: McClelland and Stewart, 1977), p. 230 ff.
10. Konosuke Matsushita, *Not for Bread Alone* (Tokyo; P.H.P. Institute Inc., 1984), p. 88.
11. Ibid., p. 86.
12. Michael Maccoby, *The Gamesman: Winning and Losing the Career Game* (New York: Bantam Books, 1978), p. 43-123.
13. Robert Greenleaf, op. cit., p. 10.
14. Kenneth T. Wessner, Service Master *Action* Bulletin, Service Master Industries, Inc. (Downers Grove: 1983).

5 Value-Based Management

1. William G. Ouchi, *Theory Z* (Reading: Addison-Wesley, 1981), p. 102, 131.

6 Community in the Workplace

1. Matt. 18:20 (NEB).
2. John 17:21 (NEB).

3 2 Cor. 13:14 (NEB).
4 G.H. Tucker and D.C. Blackwell, *Experiencing Christian Community. A program manual for Christian community development in the local congregation* (Toronto: Anglican Book Centre, 1976).
5 Donald N. Scobel, "Business and Labour — From Adversaries to Allies," *Harvard Business Review*, Nov. Dec. 1982, p. 129.
6 David Crane, "Can Sweden's Success Show Us How to Revive Our Economy," *The Toronto Star*, 10 April 1985.
7 D.N. Scobel, op. cit., p. 134.
8 Ibid., p. 136.

7 Business Ethics and Social Responsibility

1 Charles McCoy, *Management Values — The Ethical Difference in Corporate Policy and Performance* (Marshfield: Pitman, 1985), p. 33.
2 Ludvig Jonsson, "Should Firms Have a Code of Ethics?" Skandinaviska Euskilda Banken *Quarterly Review*, (3rd Quarter, 1975), 109.
3 E.M. deWindt, quoted by Charles Davis, *Toronto Board of Trade Magazine*, Feb. 1979.
4 Harold A. Gram, "The Churches and Corporate Life," *Cresset* (Valparaiso), p. 6.
5 Ibid., p. 5.
6 Eph. 5:15 (Phillips).
7 1 Pet. 4:8-11 (NEB).
8 Robert Greenleaf, op. cit., p. 26.
9 L.J. Brooks, Jr., "Social Goals for Canadian Business," *Cost and Management*, Mar. Apr. 1984, p. 2.

8 Creative Problem Solving

1 Sidney J. Parnes, "Learning Creative Behaviour," *The Futurist*, August, 1984, p. 30.
2 Heb. 11:3 (NEB).
3 John 14:12,13 (NEB).

9 The Ministry of the Laity

1 David R.C. Clarke, "Ministry, Treasures Old & New," bishop's paper, diocese of Toronto, p. 2.
2 Ibid., p. 2.
3 Ibid., p. 2-3.

4 William E. Diehl, op. cit., p. v, vi.
5 William E. Diehl, *Thank God It's Monday* (Philadelphia: Fortress Press, 1982), p. 194.
6 Peter L. Berger, *A Rumor of Angles* (Garden City: Doubleday, 1969), p. 53.
7 G.H. Tucker, *It's Your Life, Create a Christian Lifestyle* (Toronto: Anglican Book Centre, 1977).
8 2 Cor. 13:5 (NEB).
9 William Barclay, "The Gospel of John," *The Daily Study Bible* (Toronto: G.H. Welsh, 1975), I, 117.
10 Paul Lederach and John H. Rudy, *Stewardship of the Gospel: A Business Person's Perspective* (Winnipeg: Mennonite Economic Development Associates, 1982), p. 13.
11 Matt. 25:23 (GNB).
12 Eph. 4:13-15 (NEB).
13 Ezek. 33:6, Col. 2:16, Gal. 6:4-5.
14 Luke 12:48 (GNB).
15 Matt. 28:18, Matt. 7:29, John 20:21.
16 Eph. 4:1,7 (NEB).
17 Eph. 4:11-12.
18 Phil. 2:5 (KJV).

10 A Strategy for Lay Ministry

1 John H. Westerhoff III, *Will Our Children Have Faith?* (New York: Seabury Press, 1976), p. 76.
2 Eph. 4:11-13 (NEB).
3 Reuel Howe, *Centre Letter* (Bloomfield Hills: Institute for Advanced Pastoral Studies, February, 1969).
4 Rom. 12:2 (NEB).
5 E.W. Scott, Closing address to the World Council of Churches.
6 Dalton Camp, "Business Should Brush up on Ethics," *The Toronto Star*, 21 May 1985.
7 Ibid.
8 Amos 2:6 (NEB).
9 Brother Lawrence, *Practice the Presence of God* (F.H. Revell Co., 1958), p. 48-49.

Bibliography

Lay Ministry

Diehl, William E. *Christianity and Real Life*. Philadelphia: Fortress, 1976.
Deihl, William E. *Thank God It's Monday*. Philadelphia: Fortress, 1982.
Gibbs, Mark. *Christians with Secular Power*. Philadelphia: Fortress, 1981.
Gibbs, Mark. *God's Lively People*. Bungay, Suffolk: Fontana, 1971.
Hybels, Bill. *Christians in the Marketplace*. Wheaton, Illinois: Victor, 1982.
Johnson, Orion. *Recovery of Ministry*. A Guide for the Laity. Valley Forge, Pennsylvania: Judson, 1972.
Peabody, Larry. *Secular Work Is Fulltime Service*. Alresford, Hants.: Christian Literature Crusade, 1974.

Values

Baier, Kurt, and Nicholas Rescher. *Values and the Future*. The Impact of Technological Change on American Values. New York: Free, 1971.
Gow, Kathleen M. *Yes, Virginia, There Is Right and Wrong*. Toronto: Wiley, 1980.
Haughey, John C. *Personal Values in Public Policy*. Conversations on Government Decision Making. New York: Paulist, 1979.
Inglehart, Richard. *The Silent Revolution*. Changing Values and Political Styles Among Western Publics. Princeton: Princeton, 1977.
Larson, Roland, and Doris Larson. *Values and Faith*. Minneapolis: Winston, 1980.
Tucker, G.H. *It's Your Life, Create a Christian Lifestyle*. Toronto: Anglican Book Centre, 1977.

Business and Management

Alexander, John. *Managing Our Work*. Downers Grove, Illinois: Inter Varsity Press, 1972.
Deal, Terrence, and Allan Kennedy. *Corporate Cultures*. Reading, Massachusetts: Addison Wesley, 1982.
DeBoer, John. *How to Succeed in the Organization Jungle Without Losing Your Religion*. Philadelphia: Pilgrim, 1972.

Greenleaf, Robert K. *Servant Leadership*. New York: Paulist, 1977.

Herron, Orley. *A Christian Executive in a Secular World*. Nashville: Nelson, 1979.

Kanter, Rosabeth Moss. *Men and Women of the Corporation*. New York: Basic, 1977.

Maccoby, Michael. *The Gamesman, Winning and Losing the Career Game*. New York: Bantam, 1976.

Ouchi, William. *Theory Z. How American Business Can Meet the Japanese Challenge*. Reading: Addison Wesley, 1981.

Peters, Thomas, and Robert Waterman. *In Search of Excellence*. New York: Harper & Row, 1982.

Silk, Leonard, and David Vogel. *Ethics and Profits*. New York: Simon & Schuster, 1976

Tanner, Richard, and Anthony Athos. *The Art of Japanese Management*. New York: Simon & Schuster, 1981.

Vanderkloeb, Edward. *A Christian Union In Labour's Wasteland*. Toronto: Wedge, 1978.

Business Ethics

Birch, Bruce, and Larry Rasmussen. *Bible & Ethics in the Christian Life*. Minneapolis: Augsburg, 1976

Blackburn, Tom. *Christian Business Ethics*. Chicago: Fides Clareton, 1981.

Channcey, George. *Decisions, Decisions*. Richmond: John Knox, 1972.

Gram, Harold. *Ethics and Social Responsibility in Business*. St. Louis: Concordia, 1969.

Silk, Leonard, and David Vogel. *Ethics and Profits*. New York: Simon & Schuster, 1976.

Southard, Samuel. *Ethics for Executives*. New York. Cornerstone, 1975.

Stevens, Edward. *Business Ethics*. New York: Paulist, 1979.

Walton, Clarence. *The Ethics of Corporate Conduct*. Englewood Cliffs: Prentice Hall, 1977.

Christianity and the World

Kavanaugh, John F. *Following Christ in a Consumer Society*. Maryknoll: Orbis, 1981.

Marshall, Paul. *Thine Is the Kingdom*. Basingstoke: Marshall, Morgan and Scott, 1984.

Naisbitt, John. *Megatrends: Ten New Directions Forming Our Lives*. New York: Warner, 1983.

Roche, Douglas. *Justice — Not Charity*. A New Global Ethics for Canada. Toronto: McClelland and Stewart, 1976.

Sider, R. *Rich Christian in an Age of Hunger*. Downer's Grove, Illinois: Inter-Varsity, 1977.

Storkey, Alan. *Christian Social Perspective*. Leicester: Inter-Varsity, 1979.

Stringfellow, William. *An Ethic for Christians and Other Aliens in a Strange Land*. Waco, Texas: Word, 1973.

Webber, Robert. *The Secular Saint*. Grand Rapids, Michigan: Zondervan, 1979.

Work

Catherwood, Sir Frederick. *On the Job: The Christian 9—5*. Grand Rapids, Michigan: Zondervan, 1980.

Marshall, Paul, et al. *Labour of Love*. Essays on Work. Toronto: Wedge, 1980.

Schumacher, E.F. *Good Work*. New York: Harper & Row, 1980.

White, Jerry, and Mary White. *Your Job Survival or Satisfaction*. Grand Rapids, Michigan: Zondervan, 1977.

Spirituality

Mouw, Richard. *Called to Holy Worldliness*. Philadelphia: Fortress, 1980.

Peck, M. Scott. *The Road Less Travelled*. New York: Simon & Schuster, 1978.

Rhymes, Douglas. *Prayer in the Secular City*. London: Lutterworth, 1967.

Theology

Blamires, Harry. *The Christian Mind*. Ann Arbor: Servant, 1963.

Kraemer, Hendrick. *A Theology of the Laity*. London: Westminster, 1958.

Ministry and Personality

Keirsey, David and Marilyn Bates. *Please Understand Me*. Character and Temperament Types. Del Mar. California: Prometheus Nemesis, 1984.

Michael, Chester P., and Marie C. Morrisey. *Prayer and Temperament*. Different Prayer Forms for Different Personality Types. Charlottesville, Virginia: Open Door, 1984.

Myers, Isabel Briggs, with Peter B. Myers. *Gifts Differing*. Palo Alto: Consulting Psychologists, 1980.